the
FORMULA
for
IMPACT

GEORGIE SMITH
with TRAVIS BATES

B2B

Dedicated to Karen Ballantyne.
You were the key.
Go in peace.

First published in 2023 by Georgie Smith

A catalogue entry for this book is available from the National Library of Australia.

ISBN: 978-1-922764-02-7
Book production and text design by Publish Central
Cover design by Pipeline Design

The paper this book is printed on is certified as environmentally friendly.

Contents

Acknowledgements

So many people helped us get here. The best thing about writing a book is having the chance to put our gratitude in print.

In chronological order, first we'd like to thank our parents, all of whom have contributed elements to our character, knowledge and experience that, in their absence, would have made this book impossible. We're lucky to have three of you still in our lives; we love you dearly.

More recently, we're grateful to our golden era of EPA Victoria's executive team: Chair Cheryl Batagol, CEO John Merritt, and Executives Chris Webb, Matt Vincent, Katrina McKenzie and Annie Volkering. Each of you taught us what true leadership looks like, especially during the tough times.

In the same vein, to Karen Batt, CPSU Victoria Secretary throughout both of our tenures as branch president (and beyond); your character and integrity are rare jewels.

To our EPA colleagues, you profoundly shaped our sense of how to do government right. Laserlike integrity, talent, diligence and camaraderie; if we named every one of you who touched our lives, we'd need another book.

To our other staff and colleagues across the years, thank you for sharing your stories and insight with us. You are all in our heads still, whispering your wisdom in our ears.

To Larissa Brown, Jason Clarke and the Centre for Sustainability Leadership alumni, thank you for cementing the belief that service is the ultimate legacy. We hope this ranks.

To Sarah Overton, your casual confidence that we could – of course! – write a great book propelled us. Thank you also for making us aware book coaches existed, and introducing us to the best in the business.

That person being the incomparable Kath Walters; without your guidance, there would simply be no book. Your process, wisdom and confidence were the shining lights illuminating the dark days of our first and second drafting. It's a relief to finally give you a finished product!

To our wonderful reviewers, from the Ginger Beers to the Wise Owls, every one of you improved the manuscript. James Lenihan, Joseph Sanchez, Karen Edson, Scott Patterson, Jennifer Connell, Sarah Overton, John Merritt, Cheryl Batagol and of course, Sean Kavanagh. We can't thank you enough for your feedback.

To Malcolm Sparrow, for so graciously humouring a request for guidance from across the planet and for summing up the whole task in one sentence. The worth was indeed in the work.

To our amazing, and patient, publishing team – Michael Hanrahan, Anna Clemann and all of the Publish Central crew. Thank you for fielding umpteen revisions, equivocations, dumb questions and long waits.

To Karen Comer, our editor extraordinaire, thank you so very much for slashing the waffle, highlighting pearls and believing in this book from start to finish.

To Rachel Bourke and Colin Eggins of SalesSPACE, you're the reason we've succeeded in taking the next step to make Upsides Training real.

And finally, to Hugo, our very best gift to the future. It's all for you kiddo.

Introduction

IS THIS YOU?

Tell me if this sounds familiar. You want to help people, to make the world a better place. But, you don't quite know how. You chose your job in government because it sounded like a good way to make an impact. But so far it seems to be bureaucracy, rules and bugger all progress. Maybe you're wondering if government is even the right place for you.

I'm here to tell you that government is a wonderful place from which to improve the world, though it does move more slowly than you might have expected. There's good reason for that though, and slow but inexorable progress can add up fast. If you want to make a career in the public sector, you need to know why it is how it is, and how to work effectively within it. That's what this book will teach you.

While I humbly assert that anyone can gain value from the lessons in this book, it's been squarely written for young, junior public sector employees in Australia. Your agency, job title, academic background and location don't matter here. If you want to do your job well, to serve with diligence and purpose, and leave the world better than you found it, then this book is for you.

WHY NOW?

It's a truth so evident and so frequently observed that it's become a cliché – nothing's as certain as change. It's always been this way, though the pace of change is indeed accelerating.

Not all change is radical. Incremental improvement is change. Even maintenance is change – left to their own devices, everything breaks, so to keep things as they are, we must change them from time to time. **So to master public service in any form, you must master change.**

Public sector agencies around the world are filled with millions of individuals just like you. While it's executives who set strategies, it's staff who do the daily work of deciding how delivery happens. That "rubber hitting the road" delivery is where most real-world change comes from, so even the most junior staff have a lot of power to deliver change.

WHAT'S IN THIS BOOK?

This book is the boiled-down, stripped-bare, if-I-could-only-tell-you-one-thing-it'd-be-this distillation of 40 years of success, failure, observation and study. It's what a good mentor could impart to you through years of guidance. It's what future-you would love to go back in time and tell now-you, if they could.

All of this wisdom is honed into a simple, powerful equation that forms the spine of this book. That equation is the **Formula for Impact**, and it charts the five critical factors required to deliver change well.

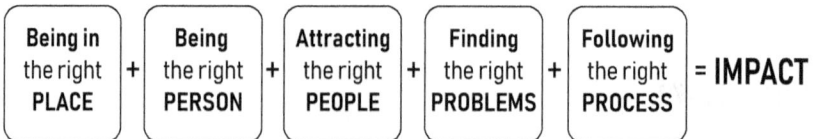

$$\boxed{\begin{array}{c}\text{Being in}\\\text{the right}\\\text{PLACE}\end{array}} + \boxed{\begin{array}{c}\text{Being}\\\text{the right}\\\text{PERSON}\end{array}} + \boxed{\begin{array}{c}\text{Attracting}\\\text{the right}\\\text{PEOPLE}\end{array}} + \boxed{\begin{array}{c}\text{Finding}\\\text{the right}\\\text{PROBLEMS}\end{array}} + \boxed{\begin{array}{c}\text{Following}\\\text{the right}\\\text{PROCESS}\end{array}} = \textbf{IMPACT}$$

The way to get stuff done in the public sector comes down to these five key factors – the Five Ps:

1. The right **Place** – work somewhere that accords with your values, and learn the rules of its game
2. The right **Person** – get your own head on straight, and become a coordinator for others
3. The right **People** – learn to muster dedicated allies and add their capabilities to your own
4. The right **Problems** – among the noise, find solvable problems worth solving
5. The right **Process** – follow a trusted method to build your reputation while taking care of business.

This book is in five Parts. In **Part 1** we'll explore why the public service is such a fantastic forum for making the world a better place, and you'll gain new insights into how it (really) works.

In **Part 2** you'll get to know yourself better – after all, you're the one person you can truly control, so let's make you (even more) awesome. **Part 3** is where I'll teach you how to harness the incredible power of other people, to achieve more than you ever could alone.

In **Part 4** we'll learn how to make sense from chaos and carve out solvable problems. Finally, in **Part 5** I'll show you the architecture of all change and bring everything we've covered together into one simple, powerful change model that will transform how you operate and make you a stand-out leader.

WHY THIS BOOK?

Great tomes on good governing exist; I've read many of them, and their wisdom has helped me become a better public servant.

But there's just one problem with them – they pretty much all speak to senior management, not staff. They assume the reader is in a position to command resources on a large scale, set policy and draw on strong networks of decision-makers.

That's great, but it leaves a gap. Management read the book, attend the retreat and come back full of ideas. They excitedly convene planning days and all-staff briefing sessions, only to have their great new ideas land with a thud – staff haven't gone on the journey, so they don't know how, don't care or worse, don't believe.

This book is different. It speaks to you, the junior public servant, in concrete, useful language that you can apply to your job today.

While you certainly don't need a corner office to read this book, it will help you build skills that will get you to that corner office sooner (if that's what floats your boat). So whether you're a road engineer, a teacher, an accounts payable officer or a mines inspector, this book will help you improve your corner of the world and have a fulfilling career in the process.

MY PROMISE TO YOU

My promise to you is that by the end of this book you will:

- understand why the **public sector** is a powerful force for good
- know your own motivations more clearly, and use those to guide your steps
- better understand other people, and join forces with them to make great things happen
- foresee and understand the seismic changes happening all around you
- feel confident to carve out problems that you can solve

- have a clear, repeatable process for making good decisions in the public interest
- make an impact over and over again, on bigger and bigger problems
- naturally get noticed and get promoted
- burst with pride at what you do!

Note – any **bold italicised** words are defined in the Glossary at the back of this book.

WHY SHOULD YOU LISTEN TO US?

This book is written by me (Georgie Smith) with a contribution from Travis Bates. Together we founded Upsides Training, through which we train public servants like you in the material in this book, and more. Travis is also my husband.

This book is the distillation of our combined wisdom. So here's who we are.

Georgie

Public service is in my blood. I was born into a family of Aussie public servants going back three generations. I also lived in the USA as a kid, where I saw public service US-style.

Back in Australia as a teen, I would sit in Mum's office in the Queensland Department of Housing after school, collating training material for the internal courses she ran.

My first proper job was in an outer suburban branch of the Queensland Local Government Department, then the Ambulance Service, before a flirtation with the private sector.

At 27 years of age, while working for a local Sydney Council, I went back to school to get a Masters of Environmental Management.

After five attempts, I finally got to join my dream agency, the Victorian Environment Protection Authority (EPA).

Good thing I was persistent, because I had a wonderful decade there. I assessed major infrastructure projects, led a huge restructure, ran a team administering 50 statutory approval types and finally, coordinated whole-of-org strategic compliance campaigns for Victoria. I use many of these projects to illustrate points in this book.

Along the way I was the head of the local union chapter and best of all, I met my wonderful husband Travis and we had our first child.

While on maternity leave, an unmissable opportunity arose outside of government. So with a full but heavy heart, I left my wonderful EPA to join Australia's peak body for renewable energy, the Clean Energy Council (CEC).

There I led the Industry Integrity division, making sure Australia's rooftop solar sector stayed safe, reliable and fair. I developed and delivered training for CEC's talented team in the finer points of regulatory practice.

Then in February 2020, exhausted, I left CEC to take a "short" break. COVID struck, turning my short break long. The quiet of lockdown helped me finally hear myself think; this book made its presence known inside my head, and my transformation from executive to author began.

While I didn't set out to become an author, I've always stood up for what I believe in, and one thing I firmly believe in is the awesome power of public servants to be forces for good in the world.

Through 25 years of working with officers at local, state and national levels I've seen the same thing over and over again – intelligent, committed professionals, awash in complexity the likes of which few outside public service can imagine, knowing that somewhere within their heaving inboxes and endless budget cycles are the means to make lasting contributions to the health and happiness of the world around us.

So in writing this book for you, wonderful reader, my goal is to hand you the tools I wish I'd had all those years ago when I started my public service journey, trying to work out how to do something that mattered. This book is written for you, to save you precious time and energy, and help you be the most effective you can be.

Travis

Travis grew up the youngest of four children in a working-class Melbourne family. His father became blind through injury during Travis's youth. This had a profound impact on the whole family; while making life harder in some respects, his dad's blindness became a gauntlet thrown down, a challenge to live life boldly. Far from retreating, his parents stepped up, forming both a skiing club and a tandem bike club for the vision impaired, competing at the Masters Games and becoming advocates for their community. Through his family's example, Travis grew up knowing that limitations are in the mind far more than in the body, and that opportunities to improve the world abound, if you look for them.

Travis has always been curious about how the natural world works, which led him to pursue science at university. After studying botany, ecology and zoology, he went to work in one of the most remote corners of the planet – the outback of Western Australia. There Travis was a Mines Inspector and fly-in-fly-out Environment Officer.

Returning to Victoria, Travis was delighted to join the Environment Protection Authority as an Environment Protection Officer, with powers greater than the police, to control pollution from industry. Then, after many years "on the tools", Travis moved up to develop and deliver training for field staff.

Travis also took on the role of union president (that's how we met), negotiating an enterprise bargaining agreement, preparing the union's submission to the biggest reform to hit the EPA in 40 years, and scrutinising countless restructures, performance managements and policy changes along the way.

Then, opportunity knocked. Travis was asked to step up to represent union members on the board of VicSuper, the Victorian public sector superannuation fund. When VicSuper merged into Aware Super, Travis was asked to go on to the new board as well. There he oversaw the management of $125 billion in members' retirement savings, defending member interests and ensuring that long-term thinking led investment decisions.

Travis is passionate about making decisions based on principle, protecting those who can't protect themselves, and leaving the world better, fairer and smarter than he found it. Now Travis and I jointly run Upsides Training, helping public servants like you to thrive.

Travis's experience and expertise have been critical in fleshing out the ideas in this book. Together we've lived 40 years of government life and collated the experience of hundreds of colleagues to distil that wisdom into these pages.

The everyday hero

This book is about making you an everyday hero, so let's start by meeting one; a humble man called Sean, who makes my corner of the world better every day.

Sean is a supervisor in the civil engineering department at my local Council. He's been there for 35 years and every year he takes the lead in training some of the "ginger beers" – the young engineering recruits, fresh out of university. Sean knows all there is to know about what he does, and he loves teaching the ginger beers how to actually get sh*t done, not just stand around waiting for orders.

I was fortunate enough to meet Sean by chance one morning while I was out walking. He'd been driving through my neighbourhood and had noticed that one of the street signs was off kilter, so he'd stopped to fix it. He didn't have to, but he saw an opportunity to make things better, so he did.

We got to talking, and I told Sean about a few problems with the intersection. He listened deeply, studying the whole area. He asked me questions that showed he was really putting himself in my shoes, trying to understand how locals used the space and what challenges they faced. I was delighted – it was so great to be listened to!

Since that day, I've kept in touch with Sean. In fact, he reviewed this book, as did his ginger beers.

And who better? Sean epitomises why I'm writing this book, and the ginger beers are who I'm writing it for.

You're a ginger beer – new to the public service, new to adulthood. The world you're stepping out into will be yours for a very long time to come. Some parts are thriving, and some parts are struggling. Whether your job is to maintain the good bits or fix the bad bits, with the right guidance, you can make a genuine difference.

Not everyone is as lucky as the ginger beers who have Sean to show them the ropes. So it's my hope that this book will be your Sean.

PART 1

PLACE

The stuff you won't get taught at work

*There is something I do not know,
the knowing of which could change everything.*

Werner Erhard, 20th-century philosopher

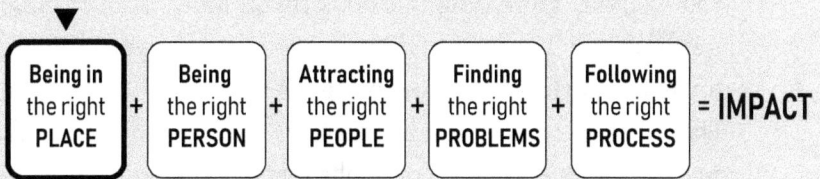

▼

| Being in the right **PLACE** | + | Being the right **PERSON** | + | Attracting the right **PEOPLE** | + | Finding the right **PROBLEMS** | + | Following the right **PROCESS** | = **IMPACT** |

Smallpox was the scourge of generations from as far back as 1500 BC. The estimated death toll for the 20th century alone is up to 300 million people. That's far more than both world wars combined.

But in 1980 smallpox became the first disease in human history to be eradicated from the planet.

We went from this...[1]   ...to this![2]

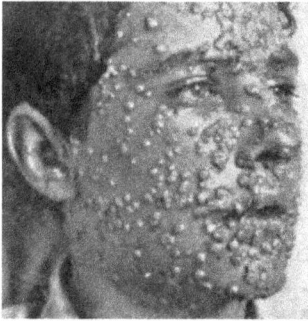

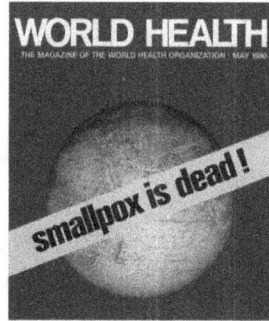

And the public sector made it happen.

The world is full of gaps between what's good for everyone and what actually happens. Every gap represents avoidable human suffering.

We all recognise huge gaps – poverty, hunger, war. There are (relatively) small gaps, too – cracked roads, hard-to-navigate grant programs, outdated curriculums. Times when things aren't safe, aren't reliable or aren't fair.

You wouldn't be reading this book if you didn't want to close the gaps around you. I see you, and I have good news for you – **the public sector is the perfect place to close gaps**.

That's because public sector *agencies* exist to do exactly that – through the work of millions of public servants like you, governments around the world close gaps every day. Do you consider yourself a public servant? If you work in an office, for a Department, probably yes. But if you're a teacher, a Council worker or an ambo, you may not, and that's okay. In this book, I'm going to use the term in its broadest sense, to refer to anyone who works for any level of government, in any capacity.

Of course, not every day can be a "cure smallpox" day, but there are millions of less dramatic examples of how public servants close gaps every day – even in the room you're in right now.

For example, the ceiling light operates within voltage limits instead of showering you with sparks. The flooring can be walked on for years without you worrying about falling through it. Your lunch is safe to eat. The clock on the wall states a time we all agree on. All those things have been made safe, reliable and fair, thanks to the public sector.

Public service isn't for everyone, but if you think you've got the right stuff, this book will teach you how to close the gaps that matter to you.

WHAT'S IN THIS PART?

This book is divided into five parts, which contain lots of short chapters. Each part focuses on one element of the Formula for Impact.

I'm starting this book by talking about the public sector, because I'm making the assumption that you're where you are intentionally, so therefore it's your **first P – the right Place (for you)**.

The ideas in this Part form the foundation of *why* the public sector exists, no matter which **level**, which **jurisdiction**, which **portfolio**, and so it stands to reason that if you don't know this stuff, you're liable to make worse decisions.

These ideas won't just make you a better bureaucrat. They should make you burst with pride at what you do, and fill you with excitement for what you'll be capable of.

This book is intended to be politically neutral. But there are two underpinning assumptions, so let's put them out there.

First, the benefits of having publicly beneficial services delivered in some centrally organised manner usually outweigh the costs of providing them.

Second, that in the absence of better alternatives, that "centrally organised manner" equates to public servants working for public sector agencies. That's you.

So with that said, in Chapter 1 we'll explore why the **public service** reaches so far into peoples' lives, and why certain things should be left to government, and other things left to the **private sector**. Then in Chapter 2, I'll help you work out whether you do service delivery or regulation (trick question – you do both) and what that means.

In Chapter 3, we'll get our first taste of power by examining where power comes from. Then I'll slaughter our first sacred cow in Chapter 4 by explaining why there is no customer.

In Chapter 5, I'll teach you the principles that will become your guiding light. And in Chapter 6, I'll challenge an idea that's probably framed your thinking until now – it's definitely framed much of the world's thinking – then replace it with a model of the world that better reflects reality.

By the end of the first six short chapters of this book, you'll feel proud to be a public servant, clear on why what you do really matters, and ready to make wiser decisions immediately.

1

Why every civilisation creates governments

The purpose of government is to enable the people of a
nation to live in safety and happiness. Government exists
for the interests of the governed, not for the governors.

Thomas Jefferson, US President 1801–1809

Empty pots make the most noise.

English proverb

Why has nobody come up with a subscription model for national
defence? So many people argue about how much defence we should
have, what type, when, where. Why not just let individuals choose
what kind of defence they want, then pay a subscription, like we do
for Netflix? We could do the same with street lighting. And police.
And tax!

The reasons why such services aren't provided on an individual,
choose-your-own-adventure basis show us exactly why government
exists and why agencies like yours are so important for solving
big problems.

THE PUBLIC GOOD

We humans, bless us, can be short-sighted and irrational creatures. Have you heard of "the tragedy of the commons"? It refers to the phenomenon where something that's everyone's ironically tends to get protected by no-one.

It's why Easter Island has no trees – back in the day, the locals cut them all down to make boats, not realising that one day, there would be no more trees.

Thankfully, over time we humans have developed the means to overcome the tragedy of the commons. We created entities to manage our commons on behalf of us all.

Those entities are called governments. Also known as the public sector.

This then is the first critical lesson you need to know. It's so fundamental that I'm going to call it The Golden Rule: **The public sector exists to provide necessary *public goods*.**[1]

Let's unpack that, in reverse. If you flick to the glossary in the back of this book, here's what you'll find under "public good":

A *good* or *service* that benefits society as a whole, which is made available to all members of a society (sometimes with conditions). Due to their *non-excludable, non-rivalrous* nature, access to public goods is typically administered by governments and paid for via taxation.

Clear as mud?

Here's the no-frills version. Public good means "the commons". It's all the stuff that's in everyone's interests for us to have access to, whether we individually use it or not. Public goods are the unsexy things that make us a civilised society.

Examples include youth mental health wards, stable currency, stormwater management, mineral deposits and even esoteric ideas like freedom of speech. All the stuff that most of us, as **citizens**, don't think twice about (til it fails).

Now because you're more than just a citizen, because you're also doing this stuff for a living, let's dig deeper into that definition.

First, public goods are what economists call **non-excludable** – anyone who's eligible can access them.

Second, they're **non-rivalrous**. This means use by one person doesn't stop them also being used by another person.

Gibberish? Let me try again.

Think about the last night you walked home down your street; the streetlights were on, yeah? You got the benefit of that lighting, even if you haven't paid your taxes, right? The lights don't turn on for some people and off for others. That's non-excludable.

Now, if I also walked down the same street, even though you were using the light, I could still use it too. And we're not going to run out of light no matter how many people are on that street. That's non-rivalrous. This ubiquitous public good is an example of the thousands of "invisible" services governments offer society every day that few people even recognise (until they're not there).[2]

The same goes for air traffic control, clean air and all the other stuff the public service administers.

Contrast that to something the private sector provides. Like Netflix. It's non-rivalrous, in that you watching Netflix doesn't stop me watching it (unless I'm mooching your login). But it is excludable – without a subscription, you have no right to it.

Things that are intrinsically non-excludable and non-rivalrous are really difficult for the private sector to provide, because there's no way for them to monetise access to it. It's the reason record labels hate torrenting!

But it's not like the government is providing torrenting services either. So how do governments decide which non-excludable, non-rivalrous goods and services to provide to their citizens, and which ones to leave to the private sector to deliver?

That's where the "necessary" bit of the definition comes in.

WHAT IS NEED?

There's an old public service saying that "every law is written in blood". This saying points to the hard truth that government **bureaucracy** tends to spring up after something terrible happens, as a way to prevent it from happening again. This is why countries tend to collect more laws over time – they're learning through experience.

Stripped back, all public service agencies are giant risk management machines. They are there to prevent or respond to risks as diverse as workplace injuries, pandemics, illiteracy, tax avoidance, deforestation or unemployment. They're there to make the good version happen (returning from work safely, being healthy, etc) and soften the blow when the bad version sometimes happens anyway.

There's a common thread to all the risks that governments tend to care most about. They represent risks to the stability of our society. Thus we can reframe The Golden Rule slightly to read: **The purpose of every public service *agency* is to deliver what their jurisdiction needs in order to thrive.**

The purpose of the public service is NOT to provide what individual citizens want.

Of course, many government services do satisfy individual wants – for instance, when my son recently got sick, I definitely wanted the care we got in our local emergency department.

But government services' purpose is not determined by individual user satisfaction; the hospital we attended was there because it's in the collective interest of society as a whole for every citizen's illnesses to be quickly and expertly attended to. The cost to society of illness and lost productivity far outweighs the cost of providing medical care, so governments provide medical care.

This same equation applies to pretty much all government programs. Unromantic, but true. Think about it – the cost to society of providing a police force is cheaper than the cost of unchecked crime. The cost of providing welfare is cheaper than the cost of intergenerational poverty. The cost of administering electrical safety standards is cheaper than the cost of dead citizens, housefires, electric shocks and melted equipment.

Now when I talk about costs, I don't just mean economic costs. I'm also referring to societal costs – loss of human health, happiness, opportunity, peace – as well as environmental costs – pollution, resource depletion, declining ecosystem health. This trifecta of costs is referred to as the **triple bottom line**, and we'll discuss that in more detail in Chapter 6.

Luckily for us citizens, jurisdictions benefit from lots of things that benefit individuals too – educated workforces, road safety rules, invasive species management, television rating systems, and the thousands of other services delivered by agencies like yours. So as the bureaucracies around us deliver all of these jurisdictional benefits, citizens benefit, too. Which is as it should be, given it's citizen taxes which pay for those services.

But never forget, the reason public services are doing these wonderful things for individual citizens is because it's what the jurisdiction needs to thrive.

WHAT IS WANT?

If the role of the public service is to provide what societies need, then who provides what individuals want? Here's a clue – another term for "what individuals want" is *private good*.

Well here in Australia (and in most of the world) the answer is – the private sector, in the form of private companies. Private companies deliver individual wants (to customers) to secure individual benefits (to owners). In other words, they're designed to make money for their owners by pleasing customers. In fact, in many jurisdictions, a company's loyalty to its owners (including shareholders) is required by law.

This division of labour between public and private can and usually does work well. The market has the strong incentive, through profit, to deliver consumers what they want, such as a new iPhone, international air flight or MAFS.

And the stuff that can't effectively be delivered through the market (because it's non-excludable and non-rivalrous) but which is still really important for a smoothly running society? That gets delivered by public sector agencies like yours, with incentives that encourage you to deliver the public good (we'll get more specific on those incentives in Chapter 5 when we discuss public sector principles).

BUT WHAT ABOUT PRIVATISATION?

Privatisation – the practice of selling or leasing out government functions to be provided instead by the private sector – has swept through many jurisdictions around the world in the last 30 years. Australia included.

Privatisation is extremely common in utilities provision – electricity, telephone, water – and in higher education. It's increasingly common in healthcare and transportation, too. Recently in my home state of Victoria, we've even seen contracts that effectively privatise the ports and the land titles office.

But given what we've just explored, can you see where the flaw in privatisation emerges?

When a private sector entity is put in charge of delivering former government services, the pursuit of profit is likely to take priority over delivering public good. It's very hard to write such risks out with contracts, and constant vigilance is required to prevent profit creep.

WELL, DON'T SUCK THEN

The chief reason public services get privatised is because that service has failed to live up to expectations until that point. You've probably heard labels like bureaucratic, slow or bloated. This is often a fair criticism. Many public service agencies are, to put it politely, rich with opportunity for improvement.

However, given what we've just explored about needs versus wants, I feel safe in asserting that the failures in public service delivery make a strong case for public sector reform, not privatisation. The suggestion that selling off a poorly run public service function to the private sector will fix the problem is like suggesting that because I don't like my kitchen, I should remove it and switch to eating out every day. Why not just renovate?

For thriving societies, **we need both public and private sector institutions to focus on being great at what they're designed to do,** rather than try to cannibalise each other. As an old colleague of mine used to say, "stay in your lane".

PUBLIC VERSUS PRIVATE – WHO WINS?

As the Rolling Stones said, you can't always get what you want. So to the extent that there's a conflict between public and private good, the logical conclusion is that public good – need – must win.

In fact, if you think about laws, you'll see that they're all constraints of private good for the benefit of public good. Laws say – "you can't speed" or "you can't smoke inside". They're really saying – "in this specific case, it's important that you, the individual, are prevented from doing what you want, so, sorry not sorry".

When there's no clash between public and private good, there's no need for a legal constraint. And if the private good is more important than the public good in a particular case, there's no moral justification for the constraint. That's why laws come with cost-benefit analyses (called Legislative Impact Assessments) to make sure that the public good benefits outweigh whatever constraints are being asked for by the law.

WORTHY RARELY EQUALS SEXY

A common argument against government and taxation is that philanthropy, or charitable giving, is a preferable substitute. The thinking goes that philanthropy allows people to direct their societal contribution where they want.

But ask any researcher trying to raise money for an obscure cancer or mycologist fighting invasive fungi how their fundraising compares to, say, breast cancer or endangered pandas, and you'll see what they already know – the popular stuff wins every time.

This is because human irrationality extends to how and where we assign value. "Yucky" or "scary" things will struggle to get funding unless someone is tasked with making a rational assessment of the relative merits of that cause versus more sexy ones.

This is why behind every government budget cycle, there are thousands of bureaucrats frantically trying to get their Minister to argue for the boring but necessary stuff, pitted against dozens of press secretaries arguing to choose the sexy project so they can get a great photo op. And guess who often wins? Most public servants I know can barely watch ABC's satirical TV show *Utopia* because it's too close to home.

Now, all of that being said, citizens still have every right to ask tough questions of governments. Questions like "why is this getting priority over that?" or "are you spending this money wisely?" or "it looks like certain companies or sectors are getting a suspiciously sweet deal from this program; explain yourselves".

And of course, there will always be debates over the exact lines we draw for what falls into and out of the **remit** of governmental intervention. "Why is government getting involved here at all?" is a question asked every day!

In fact, questions like these will drive a lot of your work, directly or indirectly. And as a public servant, you must always keep in mind that **you're spending public money**. That's a solemn responsibility. But more on that in Chapter 5.

SLOW AND STEADY

Here's the final thought for this chapter. You may already notice that things move somewhat more slowly inside government than in the private sector. It's a common criticism, and even drives many of those calls for privatisation that we spoke of earlier.

And yes, there are times when this criticism is justified (after all, there wouldn't be much point in writing this book if I didn't believe public sector functions could be delivered more effectively). However, it's important to note that the slow steadiness of government is actually a feature, not a bug. Huh?

Throughout this chapter we've explored how governments provide the things societies need, and then companies provide the things individuals want. Well, one thing that both societies and companies need is a stable environment in which to operate. That slow steadiness that governments provide is a really wonderful growth medium for everyone and everything else to get on with their lives, knowing that the ground won't shift under their feet.

Let me finish this chapter with a cautionary tale of what happens when governments perform handbrake turns on unsuspecting markets.

Back in 2013, there were some major policy changes at the federal level that related to carbon pricing. The previous Federal Government had established a price on carbon; the new government abolished that price signal soon after winning power.

Now I promised political neutrality so there will be no argument of the pros or cons of that decision; I'm going to use what happened next to illustrate my point about the value of stability.

The rooftop solar industry had been growing rapidly in the 2000s and early 2010s, thanks in part to that carbon price signal.

So when the policy quickly changed in 2013, the industry didn't have time to absorb the shock, and it contracted sharply. From 2011–12 to 2014–15, the renewable energy industry lost 27% of its jobs.

Installations of solar collapsed. This graph tells the story – from exponential growth to retreat.[3]

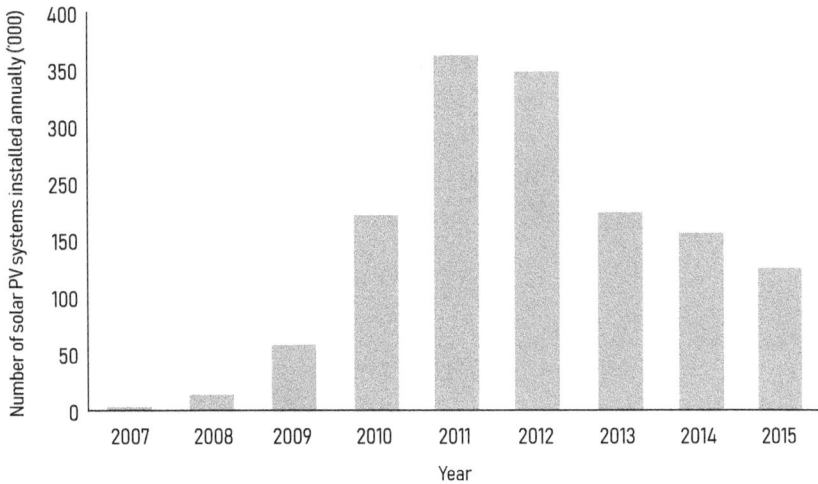

Figure 1.1: Annual Solar Photovoltaic installations, 2007–2015

Now whether you happen to like renewables or not, most reasonable people agree that sending mixed signals to sectors of our economy is neither efficient nor welcome. Businesses don't tend to perform well doing surprise handbrake turns.

So, if you're looking to transform society overnight, government may not be the place for you. But if you're keen to be part of the steady, inexorable march of progress, providing the vital under-pinnings of our thriving society, then it's great to have you on the team! Keep reading.

RECAP

- Public sector agencies are societies' way of providing for the matters of common good that can't safely, reliably or fairly be provided by individuals or by the private sector.

- The public sector provides what societies need.

- The private sector provides what individuals want.

- When there's a conflict between private and public good, public good generally wins. Lawmakers weigh up alternatives when drafting legislation to ensure that any constraints being applied to the population are warranted.

- It's important for public funding to be directed toward what's worthy, not just what's sexy.

- The public sector creates the stable environment for the rest of society to thrive. This is one reason why there are lots of checks and balances, and why change can be slow within government.

YOUR TURN

At the end of each chapter, the *Your turn* sections will encourage you to do some exercises. Most will ask you to either reflect on content we've covered, or apply the material to a project you're working on right now. If you don't have a current project, think back to an old one, or perhaps choose one you'd like to work on in the future.

I know it's tempting to skip these exercises, but don't. They serve two useful functions.

First, by reflecting and applying my words to your life, your brain is forced to form connections that reading alone won't do. **Learning takes place not when you read, but when you think about what you've read**. Have you ever had to teach someone something you've recently learned, only to find you understand it better yourself after having taught it? That's your brain forming those synaptic connections!

The second reason you should do the exercises is because your brain needs time to catch up with what you just read. So reflecting may include some spacing out, which is great! That's the subconscious time your brain needs to digest this information.

Here's your first exercise. Reflect on these four questions.

1. Did you have any lightbulb moments reading this chapter? If so, what and why?

2. Does your experience of working life in the public sector line up with what you read?

3. How does everything you've learned in this chapter make you feel about your job?

4. Do you see any opportunities to do things differently, starting now?

2

The public sector has two faces

Needs are imposed by nature. Wants are sold by society.

Mokokoma Mokhonoana, author of *The Confessions of a Misfit*

I got the inspiration to write this book in an instant, when I watched a proverbial lightbulb go off over the head of one of my brightest staff.

This happened at the Clean Energy Council, the Australian renewable energy industry's peak body, when I was heading up their Industry Integrity division. As a peak body, the organisation's original purpose was to give their members advocacy, networking and other industry benefits.

But they'd also taken on responsibility for keeping the industry performing to a high standard – that was the "industry integrity" bit that gave my division its name. I'd been recruited to help them get better at that.

So there I was, running the first staff training session on the foundation principles of regulating. In that room was Meg, the leader of one of my programs. She walked in hoping for answers, and I got the joy of watching her get them that day.

See, members had demanded that CEC do something to keep "the cowboys" out. Those members knew that shonky operators damaged the whole industry's reputation. Meg was clear that the point of her program was to lift standards in the industry.

But Meg's daily reality was that she was forever fielding calls from cowboy program participants who were also members, demanding lenience. As they'd remind her, they were members! CEC should give them what they want! Cue chucking their toys out of the pram.

This tension between what the individual members wanted and what the industry needed had been gnawing away at Meg, but she didn't have language to explain the tension. And because she couldn't name it, she couldn't tame it. We'll return to Meg's story at the end of this chapter.

Now, we're going to dive deeper into the needs that the public sector provides – wanted versus unwanted.

Some public needs are wanted by the individual **recipient**, whereas some are not. The difference between a wanted-need and an unwanted-need has a big impact on delivery.

WANTED NEEDS

When an agency is delivering a function that is both needed and wanted, we call it a **service delivery agency**. Think schools, hospitals, welfare and housing. The staff who deliver these services are often called "essential workers" and are usually fairly well-appreciated by society as a whole – if you say you're a teacher, a social worker or a nurse, people tend to pat you on the back. We like service delivery people, because we like what they provide us – wanted needs.

UNWANTED NEEDS

By contrast, when an agency is delivering a needed service that recipients don't want, we call it a *regulation (or regulatory) agency*. Think police, tax auditors and parking inspectors.

The people who administer the unwanted-needs are supported by laws to give them *power* to compel others to do what's required to maintain the common good. While many of the people delivering the unwanted-needs are shown respect – it's only prudent – they're not usually quite so loved. When was the last time you thanked your neighbourhood parking inspector?

Here's what this idea looks like in graph form. You can see how the top half accounts for the public sector, and the bottom half accounts for the private sector. As we discussed in the last chapter, the private sector is best when it gives us what we want but don't strictly need. (We'll discuss the "don't need, don't want" quadrant more in Chapter 6.)

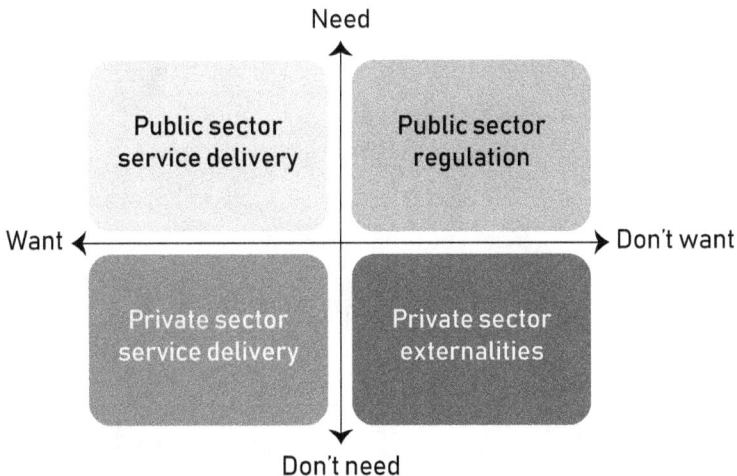

Need

	Need	
Public sector service delivery		Public sector regulation

Want ← → Don't want

| Private sector service delivery | | Private sector externalities |

Don't need

Figure 2.1: The Want/Need Nexus

31

IN PRACTICE, YOU DO BOTH

Seems straightforward enough, right? And if we're thinking in the abstract, then the distinction between agencies will do.

But, of course, life happens in the detail, so let's zoom in. On the ground every agency, and indeed every role, has both service delivery and regulation components.

Consider the example of a school teacher, delivering the service of education. Most students are at least nominally willing to be in his class and follow the rules, but there are a few who aren't. The teacher will have moments where he'll need to adopt a more "regulatory" stance in order to gain **compliance** from the difficult kids.

Similarly, your local landfill inspector isn't always in regulation mode, looking for trouble from crooked operators. She will also take a supportive, educational stance when talking with landfill owners who're trying to do the right thing, or with the passing residents who stop to ask her questions.

In these examples, we see public servants whose role requires them to switch between **service delivery** and **regulation**. They must use their judgement to know when to move from stance to stance. They may need one skillset far more often and more deeply, but must have enough of the other skillset to get by when the situation calls for it.

Knowing the difference between service delivery and regulation will help you to execute your job better. When you develop the ability to notice a task sliding from one category to the other, you will then be able to switch tactics to get the best outcome for the situation.

This book will teach you lots of tools, some of which will be better suited to either service delivery or regulation situations. So in the same way that a carpenter knows when to use the hammer versus the drill, so too will you learn when you're supporting versus when you're coercing. Both are necessary, but not all the time.

So, back to Meg's story. During the training, I explained need versus want, then the difference between service delivery and regulation.

Boom – Meg's lightbulb! She finally knew why she was frustrated – her work had shifted from delivering a service to regulating it. Better yet, now she knew how to handle all the cowboys who were asking her to bend the rules in their favour. A polite, but firm, NO.

Watching Meg's face light up, I realised two things. First, that vital distinctions like Need vs Want are really hard to work out on your own. And second, that explaining this stuff lit me up just like learning it lit up Meg. The seeds of this book were planted in my head that day.

RECAP

- When an agency or an officer is delivering a needed service that the recipient wants, we call that service delivery.

- By contrast, when they're delivering a needed service that the recipient doesn't want, that's called regulation.

- Regulation activities are backed up by laws that grant officers the power to compel.

- In practice, all public servants switch from service delivery to regulation and back throughout their day, even if their job is clearly one type or another.

- Officers must use their discretion to know which stance to adopt at any moment.

YOUR TURN

1. Write down five examples from your job recently where you've been engaged in delivering wanted needs.

2. Now write down five examples when you've had to deliver unwanted needs.

3. Reflecting on the Want/Need Nexus, which quadrant do you think your agency sees itself as? Do you agree?

3

You can't do that! Know where your power comes from

They don't think it be like it is, but it do.

Oscar Gamble, US Major League baseball player

Ravers. Scourge of civilised society...

I once found myself in a meeting full of diligent, professional, public servants from multiple agencies. We'd convened to earnestly consider how to solve the dangers posed by unlicensed bush doofs – dance parties secretly held in state forests and national parks.

To me these parties sounded like great fun! But understandably, the bureaucracy was sick of fielding complaints from sleepless nearby residents and over-burdened park rangers. Action was required.

We had agencies there who knew about public toilets. About bushfire risk. About noise (that was me). About car parking, diesel generators, overheating dancers, and everything else you could imagine a bunch of public officials would care about.

The discussion landed on a desired solution – the establishment of a permit process. Those without a permit could then be shut down by the local constabulary. Everyone there thought it was an elegant solution… except me.

Still being fairly new to my job, I slowly worked up the nerve to ask the question that seemed so obvious – "where's our head of power?"

Crickets! Nobody knew what I was talking about.

Assuming I'd flubbed my delivery, I tried to be more specific with my next question. "Which law will we use to require doof organisers to get a permit?"

That one didn't work either. I tried three or four more times, but left the meeting empty handed.

Quite by mistake, my name fell off the invite list for subsequent meetings, so I never did get that answer.

Thankfully the project fizzled out. I say thankfully not because the risk wasn't worth a response (I honestly have no idea if it was), but because I could tell that the people designing the solution were miles off base.

What made them off base? Glad you asked.

WHERE (YOUR) POWER COMES FROM

Public sector agencies and their powers don't just spring into existence. They're created, each and every one, by an Act of Parliament. Acts of Parliament are more commonly called laws.

Let me veer into Democracy 101 for a second here. We Aussies live in what's called a parliamentary democracy, meaning that the people who make the rules – the Parliament – are elected periodically by the rest of us. "Democracy" is literally Latin for "people power".

Now I know you know that – my 14-year-old nephew knows that. But just like him, few of us will ever think about it again after we leave high school.

Here's why it matters. Politicians get power because we (citizens) say they do, because of democracy. Pollies get voted in by us, and kicked out by us. And in between, we let them do stuff in our name. That includes the power to write laws, and to delegate some of that power to bureaucrats.

Bureaucrats, aka unelected government officials like you and (formerly) me, can't just pull power from thin air because they feel like it. Or because there's a need. Or because residents are complaining. Or for any other reason. They can't, because they aren't accountable in the same way as the pollies. They can only have power that's been handed to them, explicitly, by laws. Because – democracy.

So, back to that room full of well-meaning bureaucrats discussing those naughty ravers. What I was trying to establish was simply, "who says we can make 'em stop?" I was asking because I knew the answer in that case was "nobody".

HEAD OF POWER

Your agency exists because there's an Act of Parliament somewhere that says it does. And whether you're a teacher setting a curriculum, a tram driver opening the door for a passenger, a ticket inspector chalking tyres or carrying out any of the functions that our two million government officers perform around Australia every day, your job is created and bound by laws. These laws form your Head of Power.

Let's test your ability to stay awake by examining the first page of the *Commonwealth Public Service Act 1999*[1]:

An Act to provide for the establishment and management of the Australian Public Service, and for other purposes.

Part 1 – Preliminary

1. **Short title** [see Note 1]

   This Act may be cited as the *Public Service Act 1999*.

   Note: See also the *Public Employment (Consequential and Transactional) Amendment Act 1999*.

2. **Commencement** [see Note 1]

   (1) Subject to subsection (2), this Act commences on a day to be fixed by Proclamation.

   (2) If this Act does not commence under subsection (1) within the period of 6 months beginning on the day on which it receives the Royal Assent, it commences on the first day after the end of that period.

3. **Objects of this Act**

   The main objects of this Act are:

   (a) to establish an apolitical public service that is efficient and effective in serving the Government, the Parliament and the Australian public; and

   (b) to provide a legal framework for the effective and fair employment, management and leadership of APS employees; and

   (c) to define the powers, functions and responsibilities of Agency Heads, the Public Service Commissioner and the Merit Protection Commissioner, and

   (d) to establish rights and obligations of APS employees.

So in section 3 of this example, the Act establishes the Australian Public Service. Neat, huh? If you're one of the nearly 300,000 Aussies who work at the federal level of government, that's where your job was born.

There's an Act like this in every state and territory, creating each state/territory's bureaucracy, as well as their local governments, aka Councils.

Now, it gets a lot more complicated than this. I could go into subordinate legislation, instruments of delegation and so forth, but I won't. If you're in a regulatory agency, you should have easy access to this information, since it's likely to be a daily part of your job. And if you're in service delivery, you probably don't need to know.

The takeaway is this – in government, power ONLY comes from legislation. Know your Head of Power.

RECAP

- Public servants only have the power to do things because that power has been handed down from Parliament.

- It's your responsibility to ensure you've actually got the power to do what you intend to do as you go about your job.

- This is especially relevant when you're compelling others – when you're regulating.

YOUR TURN

What's your Head of Power? If you don't know it already, you need to. Ask your manager. If they don't know, ask the internet.

Hint: if you're a service delivery agency, it's probably going to come from a generalised Public Service Act like the one shown above. If you're a regulatory agency, you may have your own free-standing Act.

4

There is no customer

You can't hit a target that you can't see.

**Zig Ziglar, 20th-century sales guru,
motivational speaker and author**

In 2015 I had the dubious pleasure of being dubbed a "critically important voice" in my organisation. My prize was getting interviewed by a brand consultant who was writing us a Customer Service Charter.

From page one of the draft Charter, I saw red. What had this innocent consultant written that was so heinous? She'd opened with this line...

"The customer is at the heart of everything we do."

Here's how that should have read:

~~"The customer is at the heart of everything we do".~~

Throughout this book I'll use lots of words to describe the people you'll work with, work through and work for. In fact, Chapter 12 is dedicated to them. But at no point will I use the word *customer*.

That's because, for you, **the customer does not exist**. You have no customers. Not one. Nil. Zilch. Nada. Nyet. NO CUSTOMER.

Let me explain.

According to the Cambridge Dictionary, a customer is "a person who buys goods or services".

By the terms of this definition, if a person has the money, they can buy the thing. There is no other criterion that they have to meet. And we all know that the measure of a successful customer transaction (aside from profit) is whether they're likely to buy your goods or service again. The customer is always right, right?

But if we think back to the public versus private discussion from Chapter 1, it should be clear why the idea of a customer doesn't stack up in the public sector.

Do citizens get to choose whether to pay taxes? Can they opt in or out of street lighting? Shop around for the best border defence? Will they be given an age pension or a lung transplant simply by asking for one, or do they need to meet stringent criteria?

The public sector provides **needs**, not wants. It provides needs that meet society's requirements, not necessarily an individual's requirements. Most government programs – even the service delivery ones – have eligibility criteria and quotas.

SO, WHO?

Well, you may ask, who am I dealing with day in day out, if not my customer? I'll give you a few more appropriate labels.

They might be a *user*, or perhaps a *recipient*. They might be a **taxpayer** or a *citizen*.[1]

We might think about *future generations*. We might think about *beneficiaries* of a natural resource – like who gets the benefit of a clean river?

Then there's the *duty holder* – the regulator's version of a user. They're the ones who are constrained by regulations – the ones that the law was written to affect.

Can you imagine asking a prisoner to "please come again!"? Or asking the owner of a pub to leave a favourable review of their liquor licencing inspector?

THE POINT

Your job is not to please customers. Your job is to ensure that you're delivering what your jurisdiction needs. Because as we learned in Chapter 1, that's The Golden Rule.

You need to try to be courteous, professional and respectful to everyone you deal with – which is why I'll spend the next chapter introducing you to Public Sector Principles. But at the end of the day, you're responsible not to any one "customer" but to your whole jurisdiction. Anything less is bias.

RECAP

- A customer is a private sector concept that describes the purchaser in a transaction based on satisfying individual wants, not societal needs.

- Thus the idea of a customer doesn't fit inside the public sector.

- The people who use public services can be better thought of as users, recipients, taxpayers, citizens, future generations, beneficiaries or other terms that suit the context.

YOUR TURN

1. Does your agency have a Customer Service Charter?

2. How does it deal with the idea of customer versus user versus something else?

If after answering these questions you think your agency's Customer Service Charter runs afoul of this chapter, don't march up to your Head of Comms and tell them they're wrong!

Remember, every agency is on a journey, and fads sweep through government like they do anywhere else.

Just observe, and decide for yourself how best to honour the intent of your Customer Service Charter while maintaining your focus on The Golden Rule.

5

The seven principles of highly effective public sector agencies

Policies are many. Principles are few.
Policies will change. Principles never do.

John C. Maxwell, 20th-century author and pastor

Back in the day, I ran a team of assessors at the EPA who cranked through about 4,000 applications a year. We regulated everything from hazardous soil to the dump trucks that hauled it. We had too much work, not enough time and bugger all guidance about how to make many of the decisions in front of us.

So, for those times when the Regulations we administered left us in the dark about how to proceed, I created a two-question test for my staff to follow:

Question 1: What was the ideal outcome, from an environmental perspective? (Because our agency's mission was to protect the environment.)

Question 2: How close could we get to that within the law? (Because as we learned in the last chapter, the law was our constraint.)

Those two steps saved so much tail-chasing; here's why. They guided the order in which we consulted – we'd talk to the science team before the legal team. They decided what we prioritised when choices were necessary (which was every time). They even helped us explain our decision to those who didn't like the outcome.

Why did a little two-question test work so well?

Because it navigated one of the tensions at the heart of life, one you'll encounter again and again – the fight between **principle** and **expedience**.

Principles are so much more than just the fluffy words at the start of laws, policies and corporate strategies. They're there to set the scene for everything that happens next. They matter.

The principles I'll lay out for you here haven't come from thin air. Far from it.

Australia is a signatory to the Universal Declaration of Human Rights (UDHR) – as is nearly every nation on Earth. Written as it was at the end of the Second World War, the UDHR is a statement of wisdom learned the unimaginably hard way. The UDHR's drafters spelt out the universal principles they believed would set humanity on the right path, so we would have the prosperity that lifts us all up and avert another world war. So far, so good.

Under the umbrella of the Universal Declaration of Human Rights, most countries have derived their own public sector principles. Unsurprisingly, there are some universal principles that underpin great public service, whether you're in Australia, America, China, Europe or anywhere else. Governing is governing.

In this chapter, I'm going to lay out the top seven reoccurring principles, known as the **Public Sector Principles**.

Why are they so important? Each of these principles overlaps with the others to form a safety net underneath you.

If you stick to the principles, you'll make robust, defensible decisions that advance the public good.

Many jurisdictions enshrine their principles in legislation. Perhaps you have these principles on a pamphlet in your drawer gathering dust? What we cover here should be considered *in addition to* your own jurisdiction's principles, not instead of.

EXPEDIENCE (IS NOT A PRINCIPLE!)

The Public Sector Principles will help you guard against the biggest danger to good public service – expedience. Expedience simply means taking the easy, conventional path, without caring whether it leads to the best outcome.

Sometimes the stars align and the expedient path leads to the best outcome, so governments can get out of the way and let people get on with making the obvious choice. But don't hold your breath because those moments are rare.

We're experiencing one of those rare moments in the solar industry today. Happily, things have turned around since the crash I described in Chapter 1, and it's now cheaper, quicker and easier to build zero carbon solar farms than to build polluting coal-fired power.

But such happy cases are annoyingly rare. So it follows then that the things you're likely to be working on will involve situations where the best choice is NOT cheaper, quicker and/or easier. If it was, you wouldn't need to be assigned to it, would you? Therefore, expedience will be the headwind trying to blow away your good work.

Here then are the seven principles of highly effective public sector agencies. It's my hope that as you read them, you'll learn nothing new. If these ideas are already lived and breathed around you every day, fantastic! But please, look out if a little derisive snort of air passes your nostrils – that's a sign of trouble that we'll pick up on soon.

PRINCIPLE 1: Commitment to your jurisdiction and its rules

Deliver for your jurisdiction above all else. Do this loyally, proactively and first.

Make decisions in favour of the public interest at all times. Follow the spirit of the law as well as its letter; use your judgement to know when to follow each. Call out corruption. Speak truth to power. Give frank and fearless advice, remembering your loyalty isn't to the powerful but to your jurisdiction.

PRINCIPLE 2: Integrity and ethical conduct

Be honest, transparent and predictable. Avoid conflicts of interest – actual, potential and perceived. Strive to earn and maintain public trust. Be proportionate – apply additional effort or burden where risk is greater.

PRINCIPLE 3: Fairness and impartiality

Make decisions without fear or favour to any group or party. Make decisions on merit. Make decisions supported by robust evidence, that itself meets all of the Public Sector Principles. Remain apolitical in your work life, remembering that political consequences are a form of expedience, not principle. Embed natural justice and procedural fairness into all decisions – see a cracking model to do this in Part 5. Ensure all costs and benefits – environmental, social and economic – are factored into decision-making.

PRINCIPLE 4: Accountability

Be visible in your actions, open to scrutiny and challenge by interested parties including the public, business, media and oversight bodies. Be prompt with Freedom of Information (FOI) requests and maintain diligent records. Be timely in your decisions. Be open to constructive criticism and seek out areas for improvement. Take responsibility for errors and diligently seek to correct them.

PRINCIPLE 5: Human rights

Learn and apply your jurisdiction's human rights framework. Ensure that your obligations to citizens extend to ALL, equally. Seek out opportunities to reach out to marginalised or overlooked groups. Apply your resources to increase equality.

PRINCIPLE 6: Leadership

Seek out opportunities to improve matters within your reach, regardless of your (lack of) seniority within your agency. Be diligent and proactive in pursuit of the other Principles. Be compassionate and recognise the power disparity between the might of the state and individual citizens or groups.

PRINCIPLE 7: Effectiveness

Meet the environmental, social and/or economic needs of your jurisdiction (as relevant to your agency's remit). Plan all actions as much as is practical, then monitor, evaluate and iterate with the goal of continually improving effectiveness. Be efficient with public resources, by planning, monitoring and reviewing to ensure ineffective activities cease and effective activities continue – again, Part 5 will give you a great model to do this.

PERMANENCE

Most jurisdictions offer public servants permanent roles, making them difficult to fire. This contributes to stereotypes of lazy, inefficient bureaucrats.

But permanent public sector roles aren't just a cushy perk. They're important for three reasons.

1. Permanence enables public servants to honour the Public Sector Principles. For instance, giving impartial advice to a Minister who doesn't want to hear it is tough if you know they can sack you on the spot.

2. The public sector acts as a counter-balance to the constant changes in Parliaments. Governments can change hands roughly every three to five years; if the entire bureaucracy also changed every few years, nobody would remember how to run the show. Permanent public servants equal *institutional memory*.

3. Public sector jobs tend not to pay as highly as private sector ones, since public money must be spent frugally. So offering a non-financial incentive like secure employment attracts talent that may otherwise go private.

So the next time your obnoxious uncle slags off permanent public servants, feel free to lob these points back at him.

RECAP

- Expedience is the enemy of principles.

- Principles will guide you true then give you the ability to explain yourself when you need it.

- The principles that are common across public sector agencies worldwide are derived from the Universal Declaration of Human Rights.

YOUR TURN

1. I mentioned earlier that your jurisdiction probably has its own principles. It's time now for you to go find them.

   If you don't have them in the back of your drawer, go check in the Head of Power legislation I asked you to track down in Chapter 3. They'll probably be right up the front.

   How do your jurisdiction's principles compare to the seven principles I set out here? Any surprising deviations?

2. Identify three times when you've made a decision recently that was in line with the principles.

3. Now think about any times when you recently saw a decision that was more closely aligned with expedience. (Think back to any of those snort moments I asked you to look out for). What drove that expedient decision? Was anyone pushing the expedient option? What would need to happen differently next time to enable the principles to win out?

6

Triple bottom line versus the real world

I dream of a world where reality shapes peoples' beliefs,
not the other way around.

Neil deGrasse Tyson, 21st-century physicist

You're stuck starving on a desert island with an economist. You find a tin of tuna. The economist says, "I'll save us! First, assume a can opener."

That joke was told to me by my first-year economics professor. Another of his – "That's nice in practice, but will it work in theory?" Ba-doom tish.

Both jokes turn on the point that economics expects the real world to bend to its assumptions, not the other way around.

As a public servant set on closing big gaps, **you must be able to deal with the world the way it is,** not the way an economic model simplifies it to be (or the way a politician wishes it was).

Forgive me while we veer for a moment into philosophy. Some "realities" are not as real as others – some are more like ideas that we've all decided to treat as true.

That works fine sometimes; for instance, a $2 coin is really just a chunk of rock with some shapes stamped on it. But while we all keep treating money as real, it *is* real – for so long as we all go along with the deal, you can keep exchanging the shiny rocks for Paddle Pops.

But sometimes the concept we all choose to believe clashes with physical reality. That's when things get nasty.

Which leads us to triple bottom line.

THE BOTTOM LINE

The beginning of the modern capitalist era is generally considered to be around 1776, when Adam Smith (the father of economics) published *An Inquiry into the Nature and Causes of the Wealth of Nations.* In it he introduced radical ideas such as the "the economy" and pro-gressive taxation.

In Smith's conception of the economy, the whole point of business was the **bottom line**, aka profit. A company would sell its goods or services, then deduct its direct financial costs from the sale price, and that would define the bottom line. It was literally the last line on the accountant's ledger, hence the name.

Sounds like a pretty sensible approach, no?

EXTERNALITIES (ARE A PROBLEM)

But the flaw with this model is that **not all costs were actually accounted for**, because not all costs were paid directly by the company making the thing.

For instance, back in the day, factories that made lead acid batteries would pump out clouds of fine lead dust, which would contaminate surrounding land. This waste disposal was "free" for the battery maker, so they had no incentive to bother changing their production method.

But the cost was still there – first in the health impact suffered by anyone breathing that air or using that land (say, to grow food), and then by whoever eventually became responsible for cleaning up the lead once community expectations increased to include not getting brain damage from lead contaminated soil.

Such invisible costs are called **externalities**. Remember the Want/Need Nexus from Chapter 2? Externalities make up the "don't need, don't want" quadrant.

Some externalities are spread out over most of us – think reduced life expectancy as a result of increased air pollution.

But the nasty reality is that most externalised costs are borne by the people in our society with the fewest means to avoid the consequences (aka those with the least money), and of course, by the environment surrounding us.

In fact, many of the really big gaps that confront our world today are driven by externalities.

Here are two big externalities that exist today – you're likely to experience the consequences of both:

- Carbon dioxide pollution is simply "free" waste disposal to the environment (just as all that lead dust used to be).
- Burnout experienced by a staggering 77% of Australian workers[1] is (partly) the result of those workers providing free labour, thus externalising that labour cost from company to individual.

Externalities cloud decision-making, because it's hard to do an honest cost-benefit analysis if a bunch of costs aren't factored in. Wouldn't it be nice if someone did something about it?

THE TRIPLE BOTTOM LINE ACCOUNTING MODEL

Oh, come on, I hear you say, first economics, now accounting!

I would apologise, but I promise you, it's not as boring as it sounds, and it's building up to something important. So bear with me a little longer.

Triple bottom line accounting seeks to factor more than just the direct economic considerations into the bottom line. It says, **"Hey, society and the environment are important, too!"**

The triple bottom line model is commonly represented as three overlapping circles of equal size. There are textbooks filled with the rules for how to put costs on various externalities – how to work out the value of a dead fish, how to calculate the human health impacts of a packet of cigarettes, and so forth.

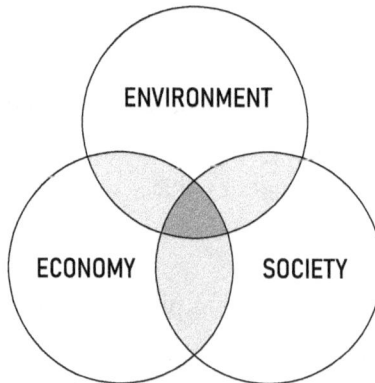

Figure 6.1: Triple bottom line model

It's a big improvement on the simplistic idea of the bottom line, isn't it?

But sadly for us, **the triple bottom line model doesn't actually confront reality.** It's better, but not good enough. Because it's still leading us to prioritise the wrong things.

UNDERSTANDING THE REAL WORLD IS ESE

I'm about to show you something rare – an accounting model that actually shows reality. I'd love to take credit for this but it's actually the collective wisdom of the mid-20th-century environment movement.

They were staring at a growing body of scientific evidence that showed humanity's growth was causing problems for our long-term prosperity, but existing language didn't allow them to adequately describe why. This model sums up their insight.

Although I didn't invent it, I have given this previously anonymous concept a name. I call it the *ESE (easy) Model.*

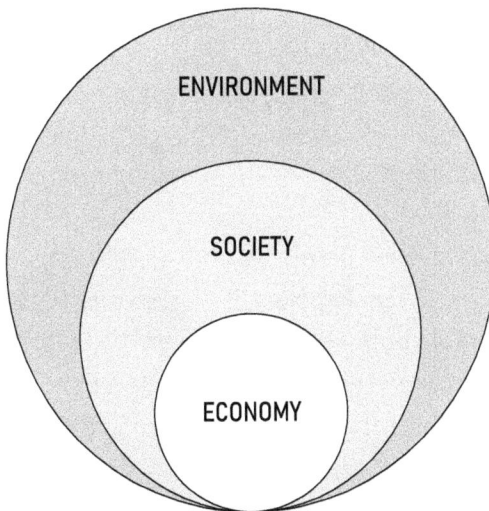

Figure 6.2: ESE Model

The ESE Model shows us the physical reality of life on Earth. Still three spheres, but now they're nested, not overlapped. And notice how they're different sizes? That size denotes how needed each sphere is in the context of human survival.

The genius of this model is that it reveals what actually depends on what. See how the economy is surrounded by society? That's because the economy is entirely, 100%, dependent on society. And in turn, society is 100% dependent on the environment.

The ESE Model shows us that, despite the fact that we generally place the greatest significance on the economy, it's actually the least important of the three spheres! And worse, that even our truly extraordinary human society is less important than the environment.

Now I can hear you thinking that this is just a hippie fantasy! Maybe you're convinced I'm some leftist eco-nutter typing this from a tree-sit somewhere in the wilds of Tassie.

I'm very aware of the danger of mentioning such ideas; nowadays, mentioning the environment means you're a "leftie", and mentioning the economy means you're a "rightie".

I promised I wouldn't veer into politics, but this isn't politics – it's physical reality. Reality doesn't care about politics at all (a fact that I suspect is mutual).

Now, let me prove my point.

Consider this. What happens if the society sphere disappears tomorrow? No more humans. Gone. *poof*

Does the economy keep going? Are the chimpanzees going to jump on the phones at the stock exchanges and buy buy buy? Pick up a hammer and keep the construction sector going? Or does the economy also just go *poof* out of existence?

And what of the environment? Does it vanish along with the humans? Or does the sun keep shining, the trees keep growing, the birds keep pooping on everything?

Rather than vanish, some may argue that the environment – the air, water, land, and non-human life on our planet – may be better for our disappearance! (Not me – I think humans, infuriating though we can be, are ultimately a force for immense good. Wouldn't be writing this book otherwise.)

But what if all the money, all the shops, all the factories vanish – no more economy. What happens to society? It'll be changed, sure. In fact, it'll be radically altered, and not in a fun way. The economy has been an incredible vehicle to improve society. But the point remains that if the economy disappeared tomorrow, humans would begrudgingly adapt and soldier on, because while the economy brings us many awesome things, it's not strictly necessary.

But what if all the air disappears? Or the sun doesn't come out for a decade? Or the soil stops growing crops? What happens to people then? What happens to the economy? We cark it, that's what. The environment supports *all* life, including us. Without the environment, there simply is no society or economy. Not even billionaires can escape this reality (though they're trying).[2]

The economy depends on society depends on the environment for its survival. That's not politics; it's reality. Annoying, impractical, uncaring, unalterable, physical reality. Bugger.

Here's where you come in.

Public servants are the defenders of those three spheres. Think about it – if you work for your jurisdiction's tax office or securities commission, you're helping the economy. If you work in child protection or hospitals, you're helping society. If you work in fisheries or forestry management, you're helping the environment.

Now, if you're a teacher or a tax collector, don't feel the need to move to the EPA – you chose to be where you are, and it's important you do something you believe in (we'll say more on that in Part 2). **Each sphere has gaps that the world needs you to close.**

Just remember that as we consider total distribution of effort, risks from the outer spheres cascade to the inner spheres.

A NOTE ON PUBLIC GOOD VERSUS COMMON GOOD

We've spoken a lot about "public good" so far, but I just need to make a point. There's a related term you'll hear in your travels, which is *"common good"*. Close, but not strictly the same. I actually prefer to use "common good", because it places the focus on the whole system, not just the human bit – a point which I can make now that I've introduced the ESE Model.

As Spiderman makes clear, with great power comes great responsibility, so it's actually up to the humans to look out for all the non-human life on this planet. "Common good" does a better job of capturing that idea.

RECAP

· The idea of the economy is a relatively recent invention.

· Nonetheless, economic considerations tend to dominate.

· Historically, only direct economic costs made it into companies' reckonings of their profit – their bottom lines.

· Externalities – economic, social or environmental costs that aren't directly paid by producers – are common to this day.

· The move to triple bottom line accounting – giving equal weight to indirect costs in the economic, social and political spheres – was humanity's first attempt to improve cost-benefit analysis.

- However, triple bottom line accounting fails to take account of the physical reality – the economy depends on society, which depends on the environment.

- Costs to an outer sphere cannot be entirely justified nor offset by benefits in an inner sphere. Eventually physical reality will impose a constraint.

YOUR TURN

Think about the ESE Model:

1. Which sphere is your agency in?

2. Which sphere gets the most resources in your jurisdiction?

3. Do you think that's the best use of resources?

4. Do you think there are any spheres that get neglected?

5. What are the signs that the sphere you work in is being encroached on by any smaller spheres, or is encroaching on any larger spheres?

WRAPPING UP PART 1

By now, I hope you feel a stirring sense of pride that the place you have chosen to work is so important. You're part of a global web of dedicated public servants who protect the economy, society and the very environment we all live in. Legend!

By learning about the first P – Place, it's my hope that you can confidently assess why public sector agencies intervene in the world. You can now identify a need versus a want, and determine whether you've got power to take action. You've acquired a safety net of principles to keep you on the right track. And you could even throw down with the next economist you encounter by showing them the ESE Model.

Are there some new gaps that you're thinking about closing now? Perhaps not quite yet, but by the end of the next Part, I reckon some will definitely have come into focus for you.

That's because in the next Part, we're going to talk about the most important person in your world. This person will shape your future. They will determine the direction of your career, and whether you get joy, fulfilment, success and wealth from it. In short, this person will decide whether you make a difference in the world or not.

We're going to spend a whole Part teaching you how to get into this person's head, to guide their thoughts and actions, to harness their strengths to help you the most. If you work out what makes them tick, then I promise you, you will go far.

In fact, this next Part will teach you how to unlock the single most important tool for a lifetime of success – you.

PART 2

PERSON

You're the best tool you'll ever have; wield yourself wisely

Know thyself. Nothing to excess. Surety brings ruin.

The Delphic Maxims, inscribed in the forecourt of the
Temple of Apollo at Delphi

Whether you think you can or you can't, you're right.

Henry Ford, founder, Ford Motor Company

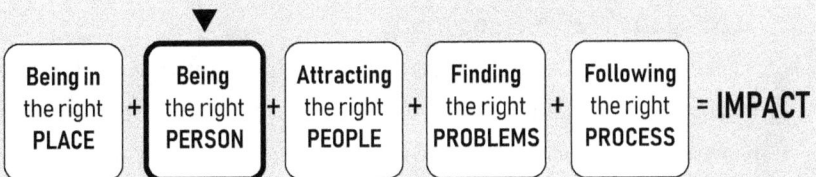

Being in
the right
PLACE
+
Being
the right
PERSON
+
Attracting
the right
PEOPLE
+
Finding
the right
PROBLEMS
+
Following
the right
PROCESS
= IMPACT

You are the decider of your fate, and this chapter will help you to become <u>the second P – the right Person for the job</u>.

Humans are an extraordinary species; we have within each of us the capacity to be profoundly wise, humble and giving. The key to being all of these wonderful things and more is self-knowledge – knowing what you offer, what you believe in, why you're here.

Big gaps are going to be closed by people who know themselves. When you know yourself, you're able to put your ego aside and be a conduit for other people, forming powerful teams that can move mountains.

Knowing yourself helps your career. It helps your cause. And it helps you enjoy every aspect of your life. **With self-knowledge, success is sweeter and failure makes you stronger.**

Finding yourself is a lifelong pursuit, and there are thousands of books, blogs, workshops and more that are dedicated to it. So in this Part, I'll show you only the tools and ideas with the biggest bang for their buck.

THE GOAL OF THIS PART

Everything in this Part aims to give you a potent gift – an internal locus of control. Fancy term for a really simple concept – people with an internal locus of control are happier, more successful and achieve more in life because they view the outcomes of the events in their lives as being *within their control.*

Let's pick that apart. I didn't say that they control what happens in their lives – they have car accidents, get their hearts broken and fail to win lotto just the same as the rest of the world. But what's different is the control they exert over *the outcomes.* In other words, how these people *relate* to what happens to them is different to someone with an external locus of control.

Here's an example. My father-in-law copped a slingshot to the eyeball in his teens. He slowly went blind, but not before years of treatment with drugs that ended up doing all kinds of damage to his body. That's enough to make many people bitter.

Him? He got married, had four happy, well-adjusted kids (one of whom I married and who co-authored this book with me), started the Victorian Blind Skiing Club, competed in the Masters Games, and to this day he bowls, bushwalks, bike rides and generally lives his life better than most 80-year-olds, let alone most blind ones!

He's a (fast) walking testament to the power of an internal locus of control. Sh*t definitely happens, but what you make of it is up to you.

So in the next four chapters, I'm going to lay out four big ideas that I've observed are the most likely to put you in a strong position to be your best self, at work and in life (because the two are one and the same).

The first idea is all about knowing yourself – the basis of your internal locus.

The second and third ideas are warnings; first about not confusing three common goals: success, power and impact. Then about avoiding the horrible fate of turning toxic.

The final idea is a technique to make the greatest use of yourself as a closer of gaps. It's all about relating to others, so forms a neat little segue into Part 3, where we talk about working with other people.

7

Map your motivations with Ikigai

To change your outer world, you must first change
your inner world.

Sharon Akinoluwa, author

You have your identity not when you find out what you can
keep your mind on, but what you can't keep your mind off.

A.R. Ammons, 20th-century poet

In my author introduction, I mentioned how 2020 started with me hitting exhaustion. The funny thing is, it finished with me finding my life's purpose. That's not luck.

I used the locked-down months of 2020 to turn inward, to work out what was really going on in my head. I sorted the helpful from the unhelpful, and asked myself all of the really important questions I'd been too busy, too tired or too scared to ask til then.

To help me make sense of the sea of questions, I used a mental model that I'd encountered years before, a Japanese philosophy called **Ikigai** (ih-kee-gah-ee). It helped me look back over my career and see clearly which parts filled me with the most joy – like Marie Kondo for life.

Fast forward to today, and those most joyful parts are what I do for a living. Working through my Ikigai led me to write this book, for you. Because reaching you brings me joy.

This is a book about work. And it's also a book about having purpose. And it's a book about making a positive contribution. And being your best. And having fun! How do those all come together? Ikigai is perfect for this question.

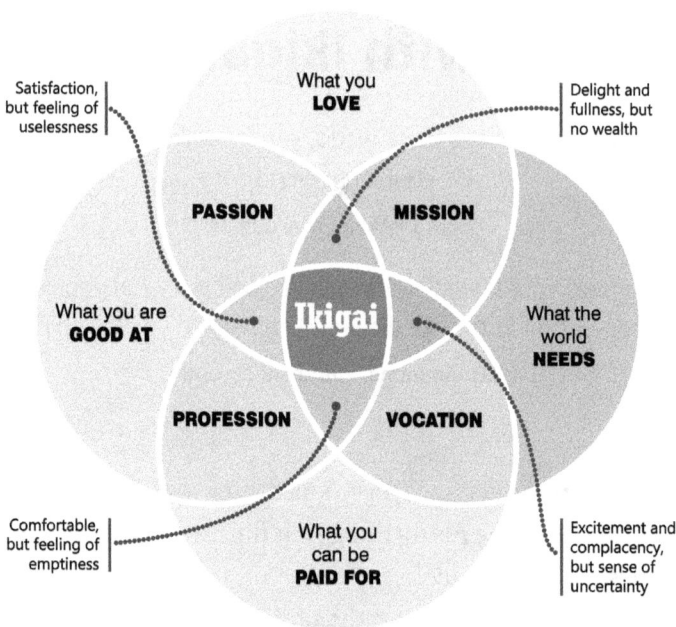

Figure 7.1: Ikigai spheres

Ikigai asks you to consider four spheres, or considerations, to form a well-rounded view of where your time is best spent. The four spheres are what you are good at (*talent*), what you love (*joy*), what you can get paid for (*income*), and what the world needs (*service*). The idea is that if any of the four are missing, you'll be in strife, whereas if you can find a job that ticks all four boxes, you'll be laughing.

SPHERE 1 – Talent

The first sphere asks you to consider **what you're good at**. These include your innate talents, as well as the skills and knowledge you've acquired so far in your life. This sphere will keep growing throughout your life as you learn.

Even when you're young, you're already good at some useful stuff. For example, in my first office job, I learned I was great at writing procedures. My brain just sees each step in a given process logically, and can put it into a written document. That was really useful for me when I was an administration officer and is still useful today – it helped me to write this book!

SPHERE 2 – Joy

The second sphere asks you to identify **what you love doing** – whether you're any good at it or not. For me, that's singing! I'm a terrible singer, but I'll do it all day long because it makes me happy. Lucky for me I have a toddler – he's a tolerant audience (even if my husband leaves the room).

There's a pitfall that's specific to passion – you may love doing something but you may still suck at it, or may never make any money from it. A friend of mine loved singing so much she went on a TV singing show, but what none of her friends had the heart to tell her was that her talent didn't match her passion. She ended up becoming the person the hosts mocked for ratings, and she was devastated. Ouch.

So, as you consider Ikigai for yourself, remember to consider objectively whether your passion for an activity is matched by your talent for it.

SPHERE 3 – Income

The third sphere injects a dose of pragmatism by asking what **you can get paid sufficiently well for**. Everybody's definition of sufficient will be different, and what counts as sufficient for you now will change over time. We all have to eat, so there's no sin in wanting to make enough money to be comfortable. The pitfall of money is that its pursuit can become an obsession. But, if you were prone to that, you'd probably be working for a hedge fund rather than your government.

Sometimes the need to earn money will trump all of the other needs. *Maslow's Hierarchy of Needs* (below) is a mental model used in psychology; it makes the point that until our basic needs are met – food, shelter and so on – higher order needs such as love, psychological safety and the like will by necessity be ignored.

Working out your Ikigai assumes that your basic needs are met and that you have extra bandwidth to consider higher order goals.

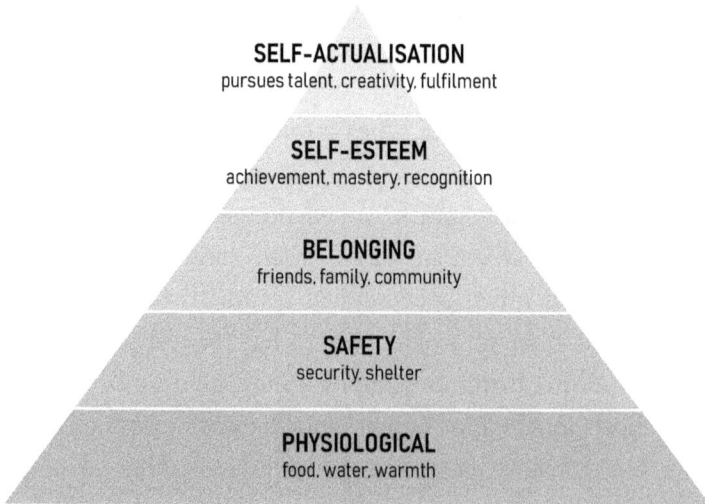

SELF-ACTUALISATION
pursues talent, creativity, fulfilment

SELF-ESTEEM
achievement, mastery, recognition

BELONGING
friends, family, community

SAFETY
security, shelter

PHYSIOLOGICAL
food, water, warmth

Figure 7.2: Maslow's hierarchy of needs

SPHERE 4 – Service

The fourth sphere is my favourite, as it invites us to ask how we can **deliver what the world needs**. Nobody wants to leave the world worse than they found it. But not everyone wants to save the whales or feed starving children either, so this sphere isn't about telling you to go start a charity.

It's there to remind you to consider your place in the bigger picture (something I reckon you already do) and ensure that what you choose to apply your energy to is adding value to someone or something that matters *to you*.

Other words that you could use to label this sphere include: purpose, values or legacy. This is the sphere where I'd be hoping to see some alignment with your current agency's remit.

BRINGING IKIGAI TOGETHER

Each sphere will influence the others to some extent. For instance, if you're good at something, you're likely to enjoy doing it more, aren't you? And we're all more likely to try to upskill in the things that will increase our salary potential.

Ikigai offers us a way to stay true to our desire to serve, as well as our desire to succeed. By using Ikigai to explore your career goals more holistically, you're more likely to find roles that are really right for you, and achieve great things.

RECAP

- The happiest and most effective people balance these four spheres in their work – talent, joy, income and service.

- The Ikigai model considers these four together.

- Use Ikigai first as a tool for growing your self-knowledge, by giving yourself a guided way to explore your own heart.

- Then use Ikigai as a way to increase your internal locus of control, by letting your Ikigai insights guide your career development.

- Your Ikigai will evolve, just as you will. Get in the habit of checking in regularly.

YOUR TURN

Time to create your own Ikigai map.

The purpose of this exercise is self-reflection. You don't need to discuss the results with anyone, though of course, you can. More important is to start the habit of consciously thinking about yourself, your life and your career. You wouldn't deliver a project without a plan, so why would you approach your career without one?

To help you start, here are some ideas.

Sphere 1 – Talent: Get other people's feedback on what you're good at. You could ask for feedback directly from your colleagues or your boss, look at past performance reviews or request a 360 Review.[1]

Sphere 2 – Passion: Think about your happiest moments at work – times when you felt really pleased or proud of what you do. That will give you an indication of what you enjoy doing.

Sphere 3 – Income: Do you have a financial plan for yourself? Most young people don't. But you probably have at least a general sense of what financial comfort looks like for you. Maybe you want to pay your HECS debt off before you're 30 and FI/RE by 40.[2] Maybe you want an overseas holiday every year. Whatever your goals – short-term and long-term – you need to consider whether your job and career trajectory will get you there. If the answer is no, then you might want to factor some additional training into your plans.[3]

Sphere 4 – Service: Consider here the kind of service that matters to you. Perhaps the answer is obvious, as it's represented by the work your agency does. If you're not sure about what kind of service matters to you, or the kind of impact you'd like to have on the world, then the next chapter, where we talk about success, power and impact, may help.

Remember that Ikigai is an evolving process across the course of your life. What you think today probably won't be what you think in five or 10 years or after you start a family or after you retire. You will evolve, so redo this reflection process every few years to keep yourself aligned.

8

Success, power and impact

Management is doing things right.
Leadership is doing the right things.

Peter Drucker, dubbed the founder of modern management

In 1986, a faulty O-ring caused NASA's *Challenger* space shuttle to explode. That day, the world lost seven astronauts and its easy faith in manned space flight.

NASA's stated goal was to continue America's expansion into space through the completion of successful shuttle missions. So what went wrong?

Despite NASA's goal, their Key Performance Indicators (KPIs) focused on sticking to the launch schedule. As a result, management got the clear signal that anything that would throw off the schedule was to be avoided.

For years, engineers at the coalface had warned that the shuttle's O-rings could fail in cold weather. But the warnings fell on deaf ears. Why? Because redesigning the O-rings would ground the fleet for months, throwing off the schedule and jeopardising success as the top brass had defined it.

So on that cold January day, *Challenger* launched many degrees below what engineers thought was safe. And 73 seconds after it took off, with the world watching, *Challenger* did exactly what the engineers had warned it would do.

America's shuttle program continued for another couple of decades. Unfortunately, the lessons of *Challenger* were forgotten, and in 2003 the crew of the *Columbia* suffered the same awful fate as the *Challenger* crew 17 years before. Again, as with *Challenger*, the ultimate cause of their deaths was the prioritisation of timeliness over safety.

What's the lesson? Those catastrophic failures occurred because the people in **power** confused **success** with **impact.**

People often treat success, power and impact as though they're the same but they're not. As *Challenger* and *Columbia* show us, the differences are critical for you to understand.

SUCCESS

Success = reaching **goals**.

Goals are most often defined by people in power (though there's nothing stopping you from defining your own success measures, whether for your job or any other aspect of your life).

Consider the KPIs in your annual work plan. Your boss told you what they were, you nodded, they got written into the template provided by HR, and at the end of the year you'll be measured against them, right?

In other words, your *success* in your role, according to your boss, will have to do with the extent to which you hit the *goals* they set for you.

Achieving success is the path most likely to get you promoted, so there's nothing wrong with seeking to succeed. It's just that success doesn't necessarily make things better – because not all goals **measure what matters**.

POWER

Power = defining success for other people.

The "hard" power in your organisation will be wielded by your bosses – your Manager, your Branch Head, your Secretary. They're the ones who define success for those below them.

Perhaps success in your agency is also defined (or at least influenced) by external voices – the Minister, the media, business and industry groups and others – who dictate what your agency does with its resources.

Hard power can also be called positional power, as it refers to the power granted by a person's job title. Contrast it with "soft" power, which is derived more from an individual's personal degree of influence, regardless of seniority. Never be fooled into thinking that only bosses have power – anyone who's ever gotten on the wrong side of their office's admin, then found themselves in Siberia, will know that soft power matters.

Your power

There's another form of power wielded by every employee, including you, no matter how junior you are. It's called discretionary effort – those small but important decisions about exactly how you go about delivering what you do every day.

Discretionary effort adds up. One way to think about all the lessons in this book is that we're teaching you how to apply your discretionary effort to maximise your impact.

IMPACT

Impact = improving what matters.

What matters varies from person to person. (Throughout this book I use "impact" as shorthand for "positive impact". Of course, there are negative impacts, too.)

We covered this above in Ikigai Sphere 4, so I hope you've got a pretty good idea of what matters to you. People can have impact through wielding power, but it's not a pre-requisite. Sean, who I introduced to you at the start of this book, doesn't have oodles of power but he has a huge impact.

So, why does all of this matter? Well, because if you aren't clear on the difference between success, power and impact, it's very easy to work toward the wrong thing.

It's pretty standard for people to simply aim for success in order to amass power, assuming that doing both will somehow equal impact. It often doesn't.

You probably know someone who's amassed power, only to discover that they aren't making the kind of impact they want in the world. Maybe they're in the wrong industry, are using the wrong skills or are working with the wrong people. These people are midlife crises waiting to happen.

But let me be clear – **I still encourage you to amass power**. Why? Because while power isn't strictly necessary to have impact, it sure helps. And frankly, most of the problems you're now facing were caused by people with power who didn't define success well and had a horrible impact on the world as a result. Just don't pursue power for its own sake, or you'll become part of the problem.

This book is training you to do it right. If you can hold onto the ideas I'm teaching you, then you'll be a better decision-maker than many world leaders! And certainly better than those who ignored the warnings about cold O-rings.

RECAP

- It's easy to mix up success, power and impact. Millions do.

- Mixing them up can cause you to pursue the wrong thing, sometimes with horrible consequences.

- Success means reaching goals (whether they're good or bad) and tends to increase your power.

- Power means getting to set the goals for yourself and others.

- Impact means achieving things that improve the world.

- You can have impact with or without power, but power can amplify your impact.

YOUR TURN

1. Look at your annual performance targets – the thing that your bosses look at to decide if you get your increment each year. Do you think that they are measuring the things that'll get your agency's desired impacts?

2. Do your individual success measures line up to your agency's mission?

3. Consider how you could alter those success measures, and what impact that would have on the results. How could you write them better?

4. If you don't have personal targets, then consider your team's or your division's targets. Are there any real clangers? I know that for junior staff it's not easy to push back against KPIs, especially if they're set across your whole team. But if there's anything that really seems to be misaligned, consider (respectfully) raising that with your boss. After all, you want to be measured on what matters, don't you?

9

How not to turn into a toxic waste

From the deepest desires often come the deadliest hate.
Socrates

Haters are broken-hearted lovers.
Georgie Smith

Many years ago, I managed a challenging woman I'll call Kate. I was new to management and way out of my depth. Kate clocked this in about 30 seconds. She once told me, "It's not my job to teach you how to do your job." I mean, she wasn't wrong but ouch.

Kate would chew the ear off anyone who would listen. She'd tell them, in detail, exactly how awful everything was. How useless management were. How the organisation was heading in the wrong direction. How the really important stuff wasn't happening. I sat right next to her, so I heard it all.

At first, Kate drove me nuts. But as time went on, I noticed something else. While she'd barely give me the time of day, Kate would spend hours each day on the phone to junior officers in other units, even in other agencies, carefully explaining the ins and outs of her area of expertise. No question from them was too dumb, or too much bother. She'd walk them through legislation, procedures, whatever it took to help. She even got nominated for an internal award, for exemplifying excellent teamwork! I wasn't the only manager scratching my head that day.

In time, I was promoted out of that office. I went on to be our agency's lead union rep, which involved me advocating for lots of staff who were in trouble for one reason or another. Talking to their managers, I'd hear words like angry, stubborn, unmanageable – words I'd used, to my eventual shame, about Kate. But talking to their colleagues, I'd hear words like dedicated, passionate, a mentor.

After working through dozens of these cases, a clear pattern emerged. They all had the same problem: they were deeply committed to their work but for a variety of reasons these staff never got the traction to have the impact they sought. **This combination of high passion but low impact turned them toxic.**

People who become toxic are wasted, which is why this chapter is so named. The goal for this chapter is to make sure it doesn't happen to you.

People can turn toxic at any level, at any point in their career. The high-ranking people control the resources. The low-ranking people deliver most of the work (and they're the ones you'll spend the most time around). Toxicity at either level is dangerous.

The worst fate that can befall someone in a workplace – short of physical injury – is to become toxic. It poisons their spirit and sours their team.

It also thwarts management's ability to execute their organisation's strategy. That represents wasted resources and lost opportunity to make that agency's patch of the world better. Ironically, that's generally the opposite of what the toxic person really wants.

Toxicity is a downward spiral. Over time, as someone becomes a little bit toxic, people start avoiding them, causing them to lose more organisational traction. That makes them more toxic, and more people avoid them, more traction is lost and so it goes until that person is so toxic they're radioactive. At that point they generally have few options – quit, get "managed out" or spend years serving in misery. That's not what you're here for, is it?

You work with at least one toxic waste, I'm willing to bet. They're obvious in any office because they tend to broadcast their distress. Think about the most toxic person in your office. I guarantee you, they will be deeply committed to your organisation's cause, yet they have failed in the past, for whatever reason, to get the impact that they want.

You probably think that there's no way you're going to become that.

Here's the thing: nobody starts out in a job intending to turn toxic. But it does happen. Ask Kate. She was a fantastic person, and she deserved better than to end up how she did.

It's avoidable though. Follow these tips to keep yourself from this fate.

HOW DOES TOXICITY CREEP IN?

Turning toxic happens in three slow steps:

1. You don't have the impact you want.
2. Something stops you moving on to another job.
3. Nasty things start happening (and keep happening).

Basically, people turn toxic when they aren't having the kind of impact that would make them feel happy and effective in their jobs, and for one reason or another they don't move on to greener pastures. Over time, they get into a rut. Eventually they turn from a bit sour to full-blown toxic once one or more bad things happen – perhaps they're overlooked for a promotion, blamed for a project failing, or their value as an employee or their values were insulted. This is the straw that breaks the camel's back, and down they spiral into toxicity.

HOW DO I KEEP TOXICITY OUT?

1. Master impact

The best defence against toxicity is kicking goals! The three-step downward slide I described above is progressive, which means first step 1 happens, then step 2, then 3. So, you can stop toxicity before it ever begins by having the impact you want.

Good thing you're reading a book called *The Formula for Impact*! Keep reading this book, and revisit it from time to time, especially when you feel yourself slipping from awesome to over-it.

2. Choose your top five wisely

This second tip will help you in your goal to achieve impact. According to self-help guru Jim Rohn, you are roughly the average of the five people that you spend the most time around.[1] So choose them consciously and carefully.[2]

Humans are social creatures, which means that it's instinctive to look to those around us for confirmation that what we're doing is right. Not convinced? Think back to when you were in high school – what were your friends' attitudes to smoking? Was it cool or gross? And do you smoke now? Did their view influence yours?

It's okay to curate who you spend time with. Choosing people that will encourage you to strive for excellence and help you work through problems constructively when they arise is a really smart move, and a great back-up plan for when your internal well runs dry.

That being said, you might not get to choose who you spend time with at work. You probably have a fixed team, maybe even an assigned partner. In that case, you need to identify their attitude (I'll give you a tool for this in Part 3), then consciously decide whether their worldview is helpful for you to absorb or not. Remember, everyone teaches you something. Perhaps they'll show you how to do things. Perhaps they'll show you how NOT to do things.

3. Self-check-in

The third tip is like an early warning system for when you're losing impact.

You can't fix what you can't see. Life is busy, and so it's easy to get in a rhythm and forget to check in with yourself regularly. But it's important to ask yourself, often, whether you're *still* aligned with your Ikigai and having the kind of impact you want. Having a regular check-in routine will give you early warning that you may need to do something differently.

Do you do monthly work planning? How about quarterly? Does your business unit have a review routine? Find something to anchor a self-check-in to, and make it a habit.

I've been doing this since my 20s and it's now so instinctive that it happens automatically. I have a little mental warning light that starts flashing, and when it does, I know it's time for me to stop and work out what's going off-track. I can't overstate how useful this habit is, not just in work but in life.

4. Have a plan

The final three tips in this chapter are all about ensuring that, when the time comes to move on, you're ready.

Have a plan. I'll say it again – have a plan. Planning is great! And this from someone who even today can't plan more than a week in advance – I drive my friends nuts. But I life-plan, well, like my life depends on it. You should, too.

A decade ago, when I was a team leader at EPA, my plan looked like this:

- Next move was to the Industry Department within the Victorian Government, focusing on supporting Victorian industry to commercialise innovations
- Then out to industry, into an ag-tech start-up, where I'd focus on securing funding for something innovative in the agricultural transformation space, like maybe biochar or algal biosequestration (gotta absorb that CO_2!)
- Side-quest over to Jet Propulsion Laboratory in California, because rockets are awesome (it was 2012; the Curiosity rover had just landed on Mars and that JPL mohawk guy was my idea of awesome)
- Then back to tech, again working on carbon drawdown
- Then …?
- End point: elder stateswoman.

Notice how it started out super specific, then got vaguer, then had a big hole in it, before ending strong? That's what real plans look like – they focus up close, then get fuzzy, but always have a clear goal in mind.

Now, five minutes after setting this life plan, I met my husband and everything changed. I still love that plan, but it was for a single 30-year-old to pursue. Today, my husband and I do joint annual planning days and quarterly check-ins. We use our big picture goals to decide who takes days off when our kiddo gets sick, which projects to start and stop, and a million other decisions.

Plans are there to shape our decisions, but not to control them. Two of my favourite quotes apply here (and by now I'm sure you've realised I love a good quote):

> As the facts change, I change my mind.
>
> **John Maynard Keynes, economist**

This quote is telling us to be willing to reassess our conclusions as new information comes to hand.

> No plan survives first contact with the enemy.
>
> **(variously attributed to every war general ever,**
> **but let's go with Helmuth von Moltke)**

This quote reminds us that even wonderful plans need to be tested in the real world and adapt to fluid situations.

Both quotes sum up the attitude I want you to have with regard to planning. It's vital to do it, as it gives you a quick strategy to deploy when your traction slips and it's time to move on.

Just don't get so hemmed in by any plan you make that it ends up controlling you. It's there to help you be strong, not weaken you.

5. Have a Plan B

If you don't have a plan, at least have a plan B.

Even if you adore your job, your team, your agency, it's always smart to have an eye out for what else you might like to do for work. This may mean a different team within your organisation, or a different part of government, or maybe even a whole different career path.

It's not about two-timing your job – you want to show up fully committed each day. Rather, it's about recognising that no job is forever and you need to know what the next step will be for you.

That step may be forwards or sideways. But if you don't have something in mind, then if things turn bad, you may feel trapped. Making a major life decision like switching jobs is not something you want to do from a negative space. If you're forced to jump quickly to the next step and you have no idea what that should be, the only step open to you in that headspace may be backwards.

6. Get good at getting jobs

The final line of defence I want you to set up is one that people often overlook – you have to be good at getting jobs. Unless you've got a large savings account, most of us won't quit a bad job until we've got the next job lined up. If you can't leave, that's a short path to toxicity right there.

I have a friend, Allan, who could write good job applications, but then did so poorly in interviews that he'd go from preferred candidate to "thank you for your application; unfortunately…"

He was stuck in a job he'd outgrown but he couldn't get out! No surprise then that he was becoming more toxic by the month, which of course was making it harder for him to present himself well in interviews. Getting good at getting jobs is a critical life skill that Allan didn't have, and things were getting dicey.

One day, Allan came to me for advice. I challenged him to start uncovering some of the beliefs that were holding him back. In Allan's case, he thought the interview questions were stupid – they didn't relate much to the realities of the job, so he treated them with scorn. I asked him whether he thought that might be showing through in his responses, and he abashedly admitted that, just maybe, it was.

Armed with this new insight, Allan set about the slow process of adjusting his attitude and fixing his performance at interviews. For him, the work was as much about changing how he felt about the process as it was about learning what to say.

So, ask yourself, "Am I good at getting jobs?" If not, it might be time for some honest self-reflection, and perhaps seeking feedback from past interviewers.

Fantastic resources exist online too, if you think your problem is more process-oriented. For instance, the Queensland Government publishes advice for all job-seekers, which is equally applicable within and outside government.[3]

Job-seeking websites are another great place to find tips. For instance, CareerOne has a four-step process just for government interviews.[4]

You should also develop the habit of seeking feedback after *every* application process, whether you get an interview or not. This will help you check whether you've identified all of your weaknesses or not.

If you think you need more help, consider reaching out to your Employee Assistance Provider. They typically have career coaching services embedded within their contracts. In just a few sessions, you should be able to work with a specialist to analyse where your interview style is letting you down and work out a plan to correct it.

RECAP

- Toxicity can creep up on anyone, at any point in their career.

- It takes three things to turn someone toxic – failure to have impact, something that stops them finding a new job even though they're not having impact anymore, and a tipping-point event that pushes them from sour to toxic.

- Toxicity is a downward spiral, as people get pushed further and further away from the toxic person.

- You can safeguard yourself from toxicity by adopting strategies to defend against every downward step.

YOUR TURN

1. Who are your Top Five, and what kind of example are they setting for you?

2. What recurring event or moment of reflection could you use as a reminder to do a self-check-in against your Ikigai?

3. What are three Plan B next steps from the job you're in now?

4. Are you good at interviews? If not, what can you do to improve?

5. If you got told you were out of a job in a month, what would you do?

10

How to become a synthesiser

Success has many parents; failure is an orphan.

Proverb

So far in this Part you've learned how to understand yourself better and avoid dangerous pitfalls. Now it's time to teach you the most effective way to use all that internal wisdom and control to close the gaps that matter to you – by becoming a *synthesiser*.

By training yourself to become a synthesiser, you will build the skills needed to unite people and gain their support for the changes you're trying to deliver. **Synthesisers make effective change makers.**

So what's a synthesiser? It's someone who absorbs information from lots of sources, then generates valuable insights out of the noise. Being a good synthesiser is the first step in being a good coordinator.

Synthesis is a creative process, and as with all creative processes, it can seem like wizardry to the untrained observer. While it is an acquired skill, it's not crazy difficult to learn. In fact, it's a lot like writing electronic music. Not everyone will become Daft Punk, but anyone can make a decent tune if they practise for a while.

The rest of this book is filled with more methods to understand other people, identify problems and deliver solutions. **Consider the synthesiser method to be your personal framework for making your contribution to all of those steps.**

So, here is the four-part process for becoming a synthesiser, which I'll illustrate by continuing to torture the electronic music analogy.

1. SAMPLE

A synthesiser is only as good as the *samples* they have to work with. By talking with the people involved in the problem you're tackling, you'll be able to get the samples you need to begin your synthesis – the knowledge, opinions, complaints, observations and memories they hold in their heads.

Develop the habit of speaking to all sorts of people. Or, I should say, of *listening*. Just as good DJs tend to collect a wide variety of sounds to mix, so too do good problem synthesisers give themselves a large array of input material by listening to all sorts of people's views.

2. COMPILE

Synthesisers need time to *compile* the samples fed into them. So the second step in problem synthesis gives you permission to let all the information you sample simply sit in your head, being compiled by your subconscious brain.

Your subconscious is a powerful computer. If you give it enough material to chew on, it'll come up with some truly bonkers connections; in fact, the subconscious mind is the source of most human creativity.

This mental compiling process usually takes days or even weeks, and would you believe, a lot of the synthesis will actually happen while you're asleep.[1] I've dreamt quite a few solutions to problems – once,

Barack Obama told me the catchy moniker for a grant program I'd been struggling to name. Thank you, Mr President!

If you're particularly adept at coming up with nocturnal ideas, you may even want to sleep next to a notepad and pen (not your phone – it'll wake you up).

3. EDIT

The *edit* step enhances the unstructured compile step by applying the structure of conscious thought. Edit your information to consider it from new angles. In practice this could mean analysing data, getting second opinions, looking for patterns, testing scenarios. The combination of compiling and editing should give your insights the rigour they need to make a convincing case.

4. PLAYBACK

Playback means presenting your synthesis in a way that's infectious to those you play it to – the right insights will burrow into your listener's ear and won't leave them alone. Put another way, this step is all about storytelling – crafting the insights into a compelling narrative.

Narratives are astonishingly powerful. First, they give you a way to check in with your coalition of support (see Part 3!) – does the narrative make them feel like their problem is understood? Do the insights ring true?

Second, a great narrative will also help you convince decision-makers to give your project the support it needs to get their backing (Chapter 26!).

And finally, once your project has kicked all the goals, storytelling helps you capture the glory, share the wisdom and get the social license (Chapter 11!) to do it again, bigger.

RECAP

- One of the most useful and valuable skills for closing gaps is to learn to be a synthesiser.
- Synthesisers train themselves to take inputs from lots of different sources and generate new insights, which they then use to create compelling narratives that gain support for making needed changes.
- Some people are natural synthesisers, whereas others develop the habit through practice.
- Synthesising happens in four steps: sampling, compiling, editing and playback.

YOUR TURN

Choose a problem in your vicinity. It'll need to be a problem you haven't started consulting on yet. Maybe it's your focus project, if you're still in the early stages of working it out.

You'll need a notebook (IRL or digital). This is a reflection process over time, so you'll need to refer back to your notes.

- Step 1: Write down what the problem is, as you see it now.
- Step 2: Write down how you'd go about solving the problem, if you were going to solve it now. You're not! But this will serve as your baseline[2] for future comparison.
- Step 3: **Sample.** Talk to the people who are involved. Talk to people not involved, to ask them their perspective. Note down what you learn in your notebook.

- Step 4: **Compile.** This is the easiest step of all, because you have to do absolutely nothing. Just put a reminder in your phone for one week, then put the problem out of your mind!

- Step 4a: Over the next week, try to pay attention any time the problem crosses your mind. Note down any new thoughts or ideas you have. This is the Compile step at work in your subconscious, murmuring in the ear of your conscious mind; while you're learning the process, I'd like you to have the experience of watching it happen. (BTW, it may not murmur at all; it doesn't need to in order to be working.)

- Step 5: **Edit.** At the end of a week, sit down and do some hard thinking about the problem. The Compile step should've changed your perspective, and now the problem should present differently to you. Perhaps some aspects of the problem now seem more or less important than before. Perhaps certain people involved matter more. Perhaps a solution is standing out now that was invisible before. Work out how you'd solve the problem now.

- Step 6: Final reflection – compare your thoughts from Step 2 and Step 5. What's changed? What have you learned? You've just done your first conscious Synthesis – how did it feel?

- Step 7: **Playback** your observations to the people who helped you get here. Maybe you want to try implementing the solution you came up with in Step 5? Either way, make sure to thank the people who helped you experiment.

WRAPPING UP PART 2

This Part has been all about fostering your self-knowledge and internal locus of control. Are you feeling more in control already? If not, tell yourself "my life is mine. I control my own fate", then go back to the beginning of this Part and read it again.

I'm serious! If you've ever done martial arts or pilates, you'll know that a strong core is vital for stability and strength. Well, the same is true psychologically. If you want to be a strong, stable, resilient and above all effective gap-closer, then you need a strong core of psychological strength. That starts with developing self-knowledge and an internal locus of control.

So as much as every single Part in this book is important, the Part that will pay you the biggest personal and professional dividends for your whole life is Part 2.

In these four short chapters you have learned how to understand your motivations through exploring what you're good at, what you enjoy, what you can get paid for and what the world needs – Ikigai.

You've seen the difference between success, power and impact. Now you won't fall into the trap of pushing in the wrong direction for you, because you've learned that being clear on the pursuit of each one can get you very different results in life.

You've explored how failure to master these topics can lead to the tragic waste of your talent by turning toxic. To avoid that fate, I taught you six strategies you can adopt as defence.

And now you've learned how to synthesise other people's wisdom into great ideas that make change happen. By now you've even started running your first synthesis experiment!

This ends the introspective phase of this book. From here on, we move to the external – thinking about other people and the problems around you. Ultimately this is a book about how to close the gaps that matter to you, and that's a team sport.

In the next Part, we're going to explore the piece of the Formula for Impact that can be the most confounding, even irritating. But it's also the single most useful way to identify problems and, even better, their solutions. Better yet, it's where you'll get your permission to act, support for when you stumble and the many hands needed to lighten the load.

Yup, it's other people! The yawn-inducing term for them is "*stakeholders*" but by the end of Part 3 you'll get why stakeholders are the bee's knees.

PART 3

PEOPLE

Because even Superman has the Justice League

If you want to go fast, go alone.
If you want to go far, go together.

African proverb

Team work makes the dream work.

Motivational saying

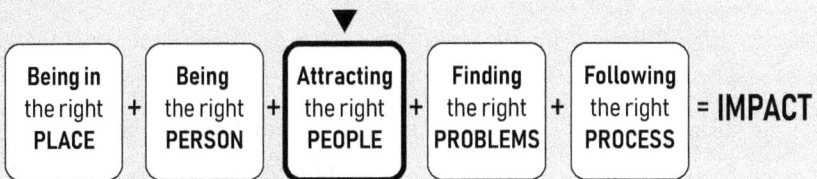

▼

| Being in
the right
PLACE | + | Being
the right
PERSON | + | **Attracting**
the right
PEOPLE | + | Finding
the right
PROBLEMS | + | Following
the right
PROCESS | = **IMPACT** |

A lifetime ago, when I was doing my masters, I got the bright idea to set up a postgraduate student representative council at my uni. Through pluck and luck, I assembled a team of powerful allies. Key power-brokers from the student union and the university faculty joined my quest to give postgrads a voice; good thing too, because I was going to need their help.

While I was gathering allies, there was one guy I totally missed. Simon was the head of the sports council, and I didn't think he'd have any interest in my project. I couldn't have been more wrong – turns out he saw my proposed council as a threat to his funding. And he had clout; hundreds of students were in the sports clubs Simon ran, and they all got to cast a vote on my project.

The day of the big vote arrived. I happened to have a horrible stomach bug at the time so I was home with my head in the toilet. I got a call from one of my allies – Simon had gathered over 200 no votes! More than enough to sink my project. I was devastated but didn't have the strength to do anything about it, because spew.

But then a wonderful thing happened. By the time I crawled back to campus three days later, my allies had handled the attack by themselves. They'd found a way to delay the vote, and had opened up lines of communication with Simon. When I asked one of them why they fought so hard, they simply said, "Our project was under threat."

My project had become *our* project, and they were willing to do what it took to save it.

Needless to say, after that we did a far better job of addressing Simon's concerns and getting him onside. The vote eventually passed, and now around 15,000 students each year receive excellent support in their studies. The lessons from that experience have helped me ever since, and now I'm passing them to you.

In this Part we're going to dig deep into coalitions of support, or just coalitions for short. Coalitions are made up of **the third P – the right People**.

So, what is a coalition of support? The term refers to the key group of stakeholders that form around a given problem *with the intent of solving it*.

Coalitions are your partners in closing gaps, the players in the big game, the soldiers in your army. They're the Justice League to your Superman. I formed a coalition of support all those years ago at uni, and they saved my bacon.

The art of forming, maintaining and maximising the effectiveness of coalitions of support is one of the most powerful skills any change-maker can learn. Which is why we're spending this Part learning how to do it.

To close gaps at any scale, you're going to need the leverage of having other people on your team. Other people bring wisdom, skills, time, money, connections and perspectives that no individual can bring on their own. Not even Superman!

Now I'm not gearing you up to be the boss here. You can form coalitions at any point in your career. When I was on my postgrad council quest, I was a nobody, and the people in my coalition were far more senior than me.

In this Part we'll get into the nitty gritty of how to turn stakeholders into coalitions.

11

Why social license matters

Right makes might.

Abraham Lincoln, US President 1861–1865

This whole Part is about getting people to support your cause, whatever that may be. So let's start by talking about what the "unit of measurement" for support really is.

Support can be "measured" (it's hard to measure, hence the air quotes) by something called *social license*. Social license is a fancy way of referring to the permission that others give you to do what you do.

With social license, you can move mountains. Without it, you're dead in the water.

WHAT IS SOCIAL LICENSE?

Social license refers to the implied permission to exist, to operate in a particular way, or to wield power. It can apply to a person, company, government, country, behaviour, religion… heck, even a colour.[1] It's not something you can create yourself; it's granted to you by your stakeholders, which is why we're talking about it now.

Social license isn't as quantifiable a thing as your agency's budget or the number of staff on the payroll, but it is detectable in the tone of commentary that you get from your stakeholders.

Social license is slow to build and quick to lose. It's also something that most government agencies seem intent on ignoring – to their detriment. It rarely cultivates itself, and "doing good" isn't enough to earn it.

WHO'S GOT IT?

In the public sector, doctors generally have the strongest social license. Makes sense; they care for us when we need them most. Looking at surveys from around the world,[2] we find that doctors are consistently in the top three most trusted professions. But some doctors have less social license than others – paediatricians have stronger scores than urologists, because everybody likes helping sick kids but nobody likes fingers up the...

On the other end of the spectrum, tax agencies usually have weak social license because nobody likes to pay taxes (even though most people tend to enjoy getting services that those taxes pay for. Go figure.) Another group at the bottom in the social license stakes are politicians.

Public servants, meaning the office-based type of government employee, tend to be about middle of the pack. Usually well above politicians, so keep that in mind when we talk about things like speaking truth to power.

Everyone has some degree of social license, including you. Yours will be influenced by where you work, what type of role you hold, your own personal performance, and the views and biases of the person considering you.

Social license ratings (there's no official rating, like a credit score! It's more like a vibe) will go up and down constantly. They can be cultivated deliberately, though I'm sure it will come as no surprise to you that in general terms, people have a dim view of initiatives that are all about raising popularity at the expense of actually getting good stuff done.

WHY DOES IT MATTER?

In practice, social license helps you ("you" here means either your agency or you personally) deal with problems and attract the right resources into your coalitions.

Strong social license gives you the ability to try risky new things. It makes you more likely to be listened to and to attract the right people to your coalition. Like Al Gore, it can allow you to call out inconvenient truths.

On the other hand, weak social license means that you routinely receive criticism and you're not believed. You're assumed to be lazy, avoidant or even crazy – whether that's warranted or not.

Social license will determine how much funding you get and what hot button issues are assigned to you for response. It decides what kind of latitude you have to take risks and to make enemies. In short, it shapes your ability to close gaps.

HOW DO YOU GET IT?

Social license is generated both by doing a good job well, and being seen to do a good job well.

Wait, what?

Doing a good job... well?

What I mean in this intentionally convoluted sentence is this – it's not enough to do the right thing. You must also do it in the right way AND others need to know that you're doing the right thing in the right way.

Think of generating social license as akin to generating happiness; it's not really something you should set out to acquire for its own sake. It's something much better generated *as a result of* doing the right things in the right ways. So just focus on doing work that meets the Public Sector Principles (and making sure people know about it), and you'll find your social license tends to take care of itself.

But if you want to get technical, we can go deeper. According to The Ethics Centre, social license is actually made up of three components – *credibility*, *legitimacy*, and *trust*.[3]

Credibility refers to how much people believe you've got what it takes to deliver on your commitments and provide reliable information. So for government agencies I'd sum that up as whether you've got the funding, powers, staff and relationships to do what you've been tasked with. For regulators, credibility is often framed as "credible threat" – do you have legislative power and the willingness to wield it where it counts?

Legitimacy refers to how much you follow your own rules and the rules set by the law, society and so on. So, for government agencies I'd sum that up as the extent to which you meet your community's expectations of you. We'll talk more about community expectations in Chapter 17.

But for now, consider how you feel any time you see a cop car double-parked or the sneering that comes when politicians vote themselves a pay rise while the public sector has a wages freeze.

Regardless of whether there are perfectly valid reasons for those things to occur, the appearance of double standards undermines the legitimacy of those entities.

You can see how legitimacy and credibility are very closely intertwined – credibility points to whether you *can* do what people expect and legitimacy points to whether you *actually do it*.

Finally, **trust** refers to your organisation's willingness to be vulnerable. Sounds weird, huh? Like, how can an organisation be vulnerable? Well, trust in governments mostly comes when you share the truth with your community – the good, the bad and the ugly.

In fact, it's my experience that this is the thing that most agencies do worst of all; regardless of any good work they're doing, they tend to be closed off to their constituents and other stakeholders. They don't say much (for the not unjustified fear of being rebuked), and so that allows people to form their own opinions.

GOVERNMENT INFLUENCES SOCIETY'S SUCCESS

Now, it can be easy to think that a failure to establish or maintain social license just harms you. 'Fraid not.

These are two graphs from the excellent boffins over at www.ourworldindata.org, which compiles data from, well, the whole world.

These graphs should blow your mind – they blow mine. They display a remarkable correlation between trust and financial health. The first graph shows a very strong positive correlation between generalised societal trust and GDP.

Country by country: Trust vs. GDP per capita

Shown is the share of people agreeing with the statement "most people can be trusted".
For each country the latest available data is shown.

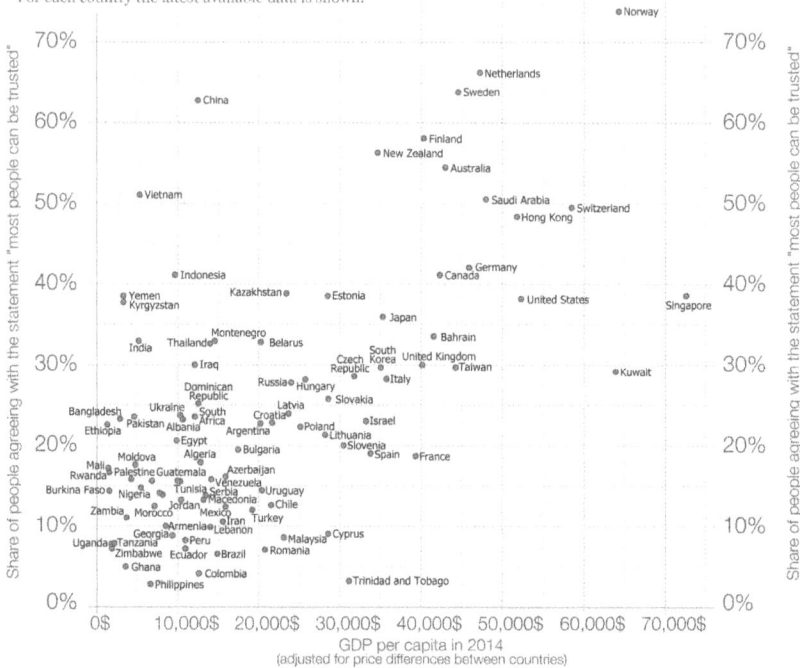

**Figure 11.1: Max Roser (2014) – "Country by country:
Trust VS. GDP per capita."**

And this second graph shows something similar but subtly different –
that there's a negative correlation between trust and income inequality.

Interpersonal trust vs. income inequality, 2016

Interpersonal trust (share of people reporting that "most people can be trusted" in the World Value Survey) against income inequality by Gini index (higher values reflect more inequality).

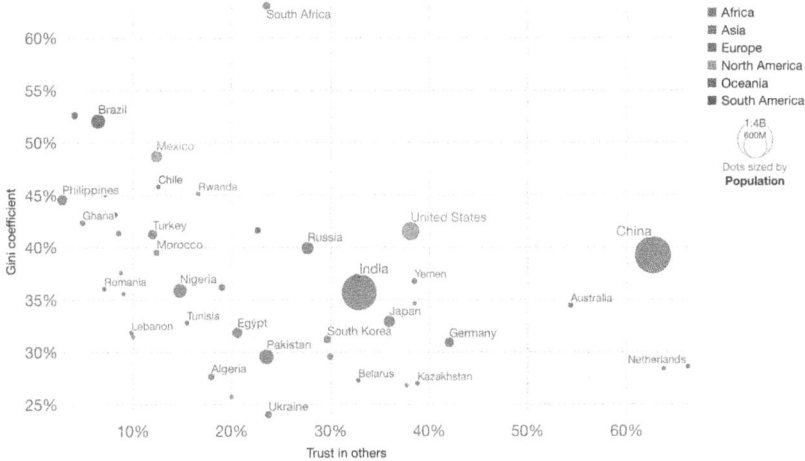

Figure 11.2: World Bank based on data from multiple sources (2014) – "Interpersonal trust vs. income inequality, 2016."

Now, it's arguable just on this data – which is the chicken and which is the egg? But, as with so much in societies, these associations become loops, pushing matters up or down together.

And are we really surprised with these results? It stands to reason – the more we can trust each other, the more readily we form partnerships to do cool stuff together. Whether that's governments letting industry join in on projects or citizens forming business partnerships or individuals getting married – all of those joining-of-forces make our societies stronger.

Governments play a critical role in forming up the trust fabric of our societies. This is due to their size, reach and of course, due to their core function. **So cultivating a strong social license for yourself and your agency is itself a public service.**

CHANGING ATTITUDES

Given what we've now explored about how social license is made, it's probably no surprise for me to point out that attitudes, and with them the social license of certain behaviours, can change over time.

Case in point: this photograph is from a "Hi, Come and join us in Canberra" brochure put out in 1973 by the Federal Government.[4] The goal was to entice young women to join the public service. Notice anything scandalous (other than those mutton chops)?

Figure 11.3: "Hi, Come and join us in Canberra" brochure, 1973

If you look closely at the pen holder in front of boss-man, you'll see it's got a girl in a bikini on it. On the desk. Of a government office.

And nobody's blinking an eyelid! If that happened today, even as a joke, you could legitimately expect to get sacked.

What other sweeping shifts in social attitudes can you think of that have happened within your lifetime? What else are you hoping happens soon? Do you see a role for government in making that happen?

SOCIAL LICENSE VERSUS POPULARITY

Social license may sound like a popularity contest, because it often is. Any urologist will tell you that.

Popularity isn't a good foundation for public administration – I'm sure I don't need to convince you of that. So what to do?

That's easy – always keep the Public Service Purpose and Principles in the front of your mind. As I've said before – these principles are your true north, your guiding light. Follow them and you'll cultivate the social license you need.

PUBLIC SECTOR PURPOSE

To deliver what your jurisdiction needs to thrive.

PUBLIC SECTOR PRINCIPLES

1. Commitment to jurisdiction
2. Integrity and ethical conduct
3. Fairness and impartiality
4. Accountability
5. Human rights
6. Leadership
7. Effectiveness

RECAP

- Social license is the "currency" that enables you and your organisation to do important work.

- Social license is slow to build and quick to lose.

- Social license is generated both by doing a good job well, and being seen to do a good job well.

- Social license is made up of three components – *credibility, legitimacy* and *trust*.

- Governments play a critical role in forming the trust fabric of our societies.

- So cultivating a strong social license for yourself and your agency is itself a public service.

YOUR TURN

1. I want you to think about a time your agency's social license took a hit. Perhaps a time when a controversy was splashed across the newspapers or when your local community members were angry because of an unpopular decision.

   Referring back to the Public Sector Principles, articulate what went wrong.

   If you can't think of any good scandals lately, ask one of your long-serving colleagues – preferably with a cup of tea in hand, because with luck you'll hear a ripper yarn!

2. Way back in Chapter 3, we discussed how you can't do anything without the permission to act that comes from having legislated power. In this chapter we've discussed a very different form of permission. How do you see social license and legislated power interacting?

12

These are the people in your neighbourhood

No one can whistle a symphony.

Halford E. Luccock, Methodist Minister

You're already a professional, so I know you know about stakeholders. You may have even been around long enough to get cynical about the tired phrase "stakeholder engagement" – I know I was! To be brutally honest, I rolled my eyes at the type of earnest conversations about stakeholders that tend to occur in government settings, right up until I started writing this book.

In fact, I have a dirty secret. The truth is, despite all of the impact I'd delivered thanks to my ability to form strong coalitions of support, I would still rather have worked on my own. I was convinced that I knew better. That I had all the answers. That if people would just shut up and listen to me, we, no, *I*, could solve any problem.

Of course, I was wrong. Ha! So wrong. Lucky for me, I'd kept my inner ego-beast in check enough to bring people along – mostly.

But writing this book has required me to unpack every last step of how to succeed at closing gaps. And the reality was clear – it really is true that no-one can whistle a symphony, no matter how good they (think they) are. **We all need other people.**

So in this chapter I want to briefly reintroduce your cast of characters from a new angle, which will set us up well to discuss how to form coalitions. Because before someone can be your coalition member, first they're your stakeholder.

YOUR BOSS

Statement of the obvious – if you don't have your boss on side, you're toast.

So I'm just putting it up in lights for you right from the get-go that you need to make it your business to understand what makes your boss tick – what do they love, hate, need and want?

Nobody has a better vantage point to help – or block – your every move than your boss. Get to know them like the back of your hand.

YOUR TEAM

The people who sit within 20 feet of you are hugely influential to your daily work, and you to theirs. Many of them form your Top Five from Chapter 9. So, study their loves, hates, needs and wants nearly as closely as you do your boss's.

USERS

This group is the one you might interact with the most. If you're in a service delivery agency or role, then your *users* are the people who receive the benefit of your service. They're your students, your patients, your passengers, your applicants and so forth. If you're in a regulatory agency or role, your users may be the subject of your controlling legislation, its beneficiaries or both.

Users can be unreasonable. You might even feel like they're the worst part of your job! But **they're also the reason your job exists**. Not only do their taxes pay your wages, but as I hopefully made clear in Part 1, your job, organisation and entire level of government exists to meet their needs.

So remember the quote that kicked off Chapter 9 – *Haters are broken-hearted lovers*. The more your users make your life difficult, the more they really need what you provide – but aren't getting it. Reframe your frustration to be a symptom of theirs, and then seek to heal it for them. You'll be amazed at where that takes you.

Oh, and if your users are amazing and awesome and you love them to bits? That's fantastic! Cherish that and help it fuel you.

TARGETS

A critical subset of users, a *target* is a person or class of people whose behaviour you're seeking to control or change.

If you're in a regulatory agency or role, then they're the people to whom your legislation applies. Your targets may be referred to as duty holders, **obligatees** or **regulatees**. They're the plastics factory owners with a responsibility to control pollution, the commercial fishers with fishing and throw-back quotas or the pub owners with service-of-alcohol obligations.

There will be willing targets and unwilling targets. There will be compliant and non-compliant targets. Part 3 will give you tools to gain insight into their motivations and guide their actions.

COMMUNITY GROUPS

Community groups aren't the same as users, though their members may also be users (or targets) – people can wear lots of hats at once.

They're important because they care about what your agency is doing, at least to the extent that it impacts the thing they care about. It's easy to dismiss community groups, but that would be a mistake. If someone cares enough about a topic to join a group, and what you're doing impacts that topic, then these people should be high on your list of stakeholders. As we unpack how to assess people's strategic value to your work, the importance of community groups' high-care factor will become apparent.

Community groups are made up of ordinary citizens, usually but not always grouped around some sort of geographical similarity. Generally speaking, they're made up of people with their personal hats on, not their business hats (see sidebar on Hats). They might be friends of the local creek or they might be parents of the students at your local school. Alternatively, they may be an online group, such as Fortnite players or signatories to an e-petition.

HATS

When I say "hats", I'm referring to the identities or roles that people adopt at any given moment. We all wear lots of hats – I'm a mother, wife, author, member of a couple of community groups, op shop hound, serial renovator... the list goes on. You also wear lots of hats. I bet you could come up with 10 right now.

Hats matter, because your stakeholders wear many, simultaneously, and their view of the world (and of you) will be filtered through their hats. You need to identify their hats, and if necessary, specify to them which hat you're speaking to when you engage with them.

If you ever get a weird response from someone, it could be because you think you're speaking to one of their hats but they're responding through another one.

BUSINESS AND INDUSTRY

This category includes individual business as well as peak bodies (groups that represent their industries). This category can also include groupings such as all of the businesses in a particular area, like an industrial park or high street.

While businesses are ultimately made up of individual humans, those individuals behave differently when they're wearing their work hat. Their priorities, values and pressures change – often dramatically. In business, people can suffer from diffused responsibility. This is sometimes called the Nuremburg Defence, so named after the "I was just following orders" excuse most infamously used by Nazis in the Nuremberg war crimes trials after WWII.

Today it's still common for employees to simply follow orders, or even company culture, without applying their own personal judgement. Modern examples include Enron traders causing huge blackouts to drive up profits, or Volkswagen programming their diesel cars to cheat emissions tests rather than drive cleanly.

By the way, the Nuremberg court decided that the "following orders" defence lessened, but didn't excuse, responsibility for those war atrocities. The lesson they wanted the world to take from it is that everyone has a responsibility to do what's right, even if your job is at stake.

ELECTED OFFICIALS

You're in government, so you probably understand more about the role of elected officials than they may do themselves. Elected officials are the yin to your yang, in that they're also part of this amorphous blob people call "government" (even if they're sitting on the opposition benches).

However, as you know; you're designed to be permanent, stable, and to give the same frank and fearless advice no matter who is in power.

But as you also know, elected officials are the opposite – they can be un-elected if they stuff up. In fact, they're designed to be directly, pointedly, accountable to the (voting) public every three-to-fiveish years.

Now so far I probably haven't told you anything you didn't already know about pollies, but I just need to set down the foundations before making my point. Bear with me for one more paragraph of preamble.

Elected officials of all stripes will be super focused on what the media says about their portfolio's performance because the media is both a measure of, and setter of, public sentiment. This means that all but the most exceptional politician will have a shorter-term view than you will.

What does this mean for you in practice? Especially early in your career, when you're vanishingly unlikely to ever even be in the same room as a pollie, let alone be briefing them? Well, the first thing to note is that they will have a finely tuned risk radar, so may be unwilling to support radical or novel ideas, no matter how much evidence there is behind them.

However, do remember that politicians can also be breathtakingly brave when the time is right. I've seen transformative politicians challenge agencies to be bolder than they've ever been, to think 20 or even 50 years in the future,[1] and to bring in life-changing legislation whose impact rings down the generations.[2]

In the junior ranks, you can get away with having only a vague idea of the specific political climate you're in. But the more your work involves projects that touch on hot-button issues, or the higher you go, the more aware you need to be of what's happening in the political sphere. We'll talk more in Part 4 about ways to scan your environment for information.

THE MEDIA

The media is often referred to as the fourth estate. Its nominal role is to report on the goings-on of the rest of the world. However, it's self-evident that the media also has the power to shape the world around it, by choosing what to report and how to report it.

Some media, such as our ABC, is state-run, which means it gets its operating budget through government allocation just the same as your agency does, and thus has obligations to deliver local news content. Non-state-run media is funded through commercial revenue – subscriptions and one-off sales of newspapers, streaming services, and of course, advertising.

There is a general consensus that "a free press is a good press", meaning that journalists should be free to report the truth as they find it, without fear or favour (just like you). Traditionally this freedom meant keeping out undue influence from government officials, through more recently it's expanded to include fear of capture from media owners, special interest groups or large corporate advertisers.

In some countries (such as Australia), media ownership is concentrated to such an extent that we're now seeing widespread calls (including from former Aussie Prime Ministers Rudd and Turnbull) for greater media diversity, because the lack thereof is feared to be warping our political discourse.

Now, the term "media" usually calls to mind large mastheads or corporations, but it also includes a plethora of smaller sources – your local community radio stations, community TV channels, small-town newspapers, industry magazines, and special interest periodicals all form part of the media landscape, too. These are sources far more likely to want to hear about a promising government project affecting their niche audience, so they're good places to keep on your radar when the time comes to get your message out to the community (via your Communications team, if you have one. They tend to get shirty when staff speak to the media unsupervised).

And I'd be remiss if I didn't mention "the fifth estate" – the non-traditional media proliferating on the internet, from social media to blogs to fringe media outlets. Often filled with user-generated content, social media and the rest is now exerting a huge and poorly understood influence over modern thinking.

What all of this means for you will depend largely on two things. First, the extent to which your work brushes up against (or perhaps firmly grabs on to) controversial topics. Second, the extent to which you'll use the media (fourth or fifth estates) as one of your many levers of change.

BLAST

It's not enough to do good. **In order to build social license, you must also be seen to do good.**

Every contact with every stakeholder is a chance to be seen to do good. However, direct stakeholder contact can be hard to scale.

Depending on the gap you're trying to close, you might need to work out other ways to put your message on blast. Here are a few tips (but again, proceed via your Comms team!):

- Use your organisation's channels, for example, newsletters, email blasts, social media.
- Ask coalition members to promote key messages through their channels.
- Issue press releases and follow them up with direct calls to journalists, especially those in the niche publications that might be most interested in your message.

RECAP

- Stakeholders are like extra superheroes – they each have their own unique powers and you want to get them onto your team.
- Coalitions of support are stakeholders who've joined your team to solve the problem you're working on.
- There are lots of different types of stakeholders, and we all wear multiple hats.
- When dealing with people, keep an eye on which hat you're talking to them through and check whether they realise that. If they're responding through a different hat, you can have a warped conversation.
- It's not enough to do good. In order to build social license, you must also be seen to do good. Stakeholders offer excellent means to amplify your message.

YOUR TURN

1. The list above doesn't capture all stakeholder groups. Think about the stakeholders you deal with most – what categories do they fall into? Have I missed any of your big ones?

2. Do any of your stakeholders or stakeholder groups scare you? Intimidate you? Make you groan just at the thought of engaging? Try to pin down why that is (if you're stumped, the HEAT model I'll show you in the next chapter should help).

3. What could you do about that point of friction? Which other stakeholders might be able to shed light on a way forward?

13

Learn how to take people's temperature with HEAT

Seek first to understand, then to be understood.

Stephen Covey, author, *The 7 Habits of Highly Effective People*

Soon, I'm going to give you two tools to help you analyse your stakeholders on a whole new level. Both tools track the four elements experience has taught me are the most valuable: *Heft*, *Engagement*, *Attitude* and *Trigger* – *HEAT*. So before I show you the tools, let me fill you in on HEAT.

Remember Simon, the guy who tried to kill off my postgrad council back at the start of this Part? Simon's a great example of the risk of not properly considering a stakeholder's HEAT. He had lots of heft, lots of engagement, a very negative attitude and his trigger well and truly got pulled by my project. I didn't get to know him well enough to learn his trigger – if I had, I never would've ignored his heft and engagement like I did.

I've always been grateful for that experience. Because hoo boy, did it ever underline the power of HEAT! Unintentionally, he made me a better change-maker. Thanks, Simon.

By the way, did you see what happened there? I was grateful to the guy who tried to blow up my project. That doesn't make me a saint! It makes me someone with an internal locus of control. It's a great example of taking responsibility for the *outcome* of events. The outcome of that stuff-up, for me, was that I learned a really important life lesson that has saved me from stuffing up much more important projects. That's the power of internal locus!

HEFT

Heft refers to the *level of influence* each stakeholder or stakeholder group has on your project.

An individual member of the community, for instance, would probably not have much heft, unless they're also the head of the Parents Association or the cousin of the police chief. A journalist who writes about your agency, on the other hand, is likely to have a lot of heft. Heft tends to be a static rating, as it generally won't change much across the life of a project. However, this can change if someone leaves their role or moves away.

It's a bit brutal, but the reality is that heft is the first element on the list because it's the single most important one to track. If you have two people who hate your project – one is the Minister's senior aide and the other is a retired bus driver, which one do you care about more?

I don't want to suggest you ignore anyone – **there's no such thing as a valueless stakeholder** – but your energy is finite, so heft is a good way to prioritise.

ENGAGEMENT

Engagement refers to the stakeholder's *degree of interest* in your project, or the problem that the project is targeting. **Engagement, unlike heft, is susceptible to change without notice.**

Recently I was browsing a local business group I'm in, idly checking out the various posts about what services people provided. My eyes fell upon one that spoke about printing training material – a topic close to my heart, as I am planning to turn this book into courses (you should absolutely tell your boss about this). Well, in an instant my engagement went from about 5 per cent to 100 per cent.

Assessing changes in engagement, especially along with changes in attitude (next), can give you a useful indicator of how your project is progressing. Engagement is detectable in metrics like website hits, newspaper article inches, trending topics on the socials, phone calls and meeting attendance.

But always remember to consider engagement *with* attitude. Not all engagement is positive...

ATTITUDE

By now you may have worked out that **attitude** refers to the stakeholder's *disposition* to your project or the problem you're tackling. In simple terms, do they love you or hate you?

In the next chapter we'll track attitude using four categories – hostile, neutral, supportive, unknown – but you can break this out into as many categories as you want. (On a particularly gnarly project, I used eight categories: irate, angry, concerned, hesitant, neutral, supportive, enthusiastic and cheerleader.)

Pairing attitude with engagement makes perfect sense when you think about it. Engagement or attitude alone only tell you so much. You need both to really get a handle on what you're dealing with.

Imagine someone in a koala suit asking 100 passers-by what they think about saving native habitat. Is anyone really going to say, "log it all!"? Hardly. But, of those same 100 supposed tree-lovers, how many are going to sign on the nice koala's clipboard to commit to a donation? Positive attitude but low engagement.

Conversely, imagine on the next corner there's a bloke in a leather jacket offering those same passers-by the chance to take a test drive of his shiny new car. Out of those 100 people, how many do you reckon will be very interested to hear more, even if their scepticism is dialled up to 11? High engagement, undecided attitude.

Now what if the koala turned out to be Bob Brown, or the guy with the car was actually Elon Musk? That's some heft. How do you think that would change people's engagement and attitude scores?

TRIGGER

Trigger – this final element is particularly nifty, because it's the one that allows you to change a stakeholder's interest or attitude. Unlike the other three criteria, trigger isn't a sliding scale from one extreme to another, but rather it's a topic or focus point. Trigger refers to *the thing/s that the stakeholder really cares about*, and thus, the thing/s you can focus on when you're trying to improve their interest or attitude toward your project.

The great news is that working out triggers can be easy – just ask! Most people will tell you all about what matters to them. Or what bugs them. Or where their headaches are. Your job is to learn to hear what they're saying (and what they're *really* saying), then reframe your project into a solution to *their* problem.

Now, when I say to reframe, I don't mean to change your project or to tell fibs to anyone! Reframing means pointing out how your project solves a given problem. Projects solve lots of problems, and you don't need to talk about every solution with every person. Reframing is about tailoring your message to your listener, that's all.

RECAP

- When engaging with your stakeholders, it helps to have a framework to guide your contemplation of them.

- Use HEAT – heft, engagement, attitude, trigger – to "take their temperature".

- Heft is fairly static.

- Engagement and attitude can change in an instant. They should generally be considered together, as either score on its own only tells part of the picture.

- Triggers can be used to change people's engagement and attitude.

YOUR TURN

1. Who are your top three heftiest stakeholders or stakeholder groups right now?

2. Who's got the highest engagement of those three? The lowest? Have any of them changed over time?

3. Where does each one fall, on a love-ya/hate-ya attitude spectrum? Again, do you notice any big changes?

4. What are their triggers? Did any of them have a change in engagement or attitude due to one of their triggers getting pulled?

Doing a quick thought exercise like the one above is fine for just a few stakeholders. But the reality of real-world government projects is that you've rarely got just a single-digit list. And to really make the most of the possibilities open to you to add stakeholders to your coalitions (as well as head off surprise Simon attacks like I suffered), you'll need to dial up the rigour from time to time.

14

The HEAT Sheet

Life is long and the world is small.

Proverb

The HEAT Sheet gives you a way to capture and analyse critical information about lots of stakeholders in a straightforward spreadsheet.

I know, I know – spreadsheets, boring. But not this time; the bigger your projects become, the harder it is to hold it all in your head. So by dumping it on a page, you'll be surprised at the insights that jump out at you. Remember – insights are chances to close gaps!

So here's how we generate a HEAT Sheet – we State, Rate, Contemplate, Correct. (Don't you think "contemplate correct" sounds like something an '80s rapper might say? Maybe that's just me.)

STATE

You can't make a stakeholder spreadsheet without a list of your stakeholders, can you? So first, you need to **state** who each stakeholder is.

A word of caution for those thinking "duh" at this point: I know that 90% of the list is already in your head. It's the 10% you fail to identify that'll bite you – cough, Simon.

You can save yourself the proverbial tetanus shot by pulling together your stakeholder list with project colleagues if possible. That'll make sure you don't overlook anyone. If in doubt, add 'em.

Stakeholder
Stakeholder 1
Stakeholder 2
Stakeholder 3
Stakeholder 4

Figure 14.1: HEAT Sheet state step

RATE

Once you know who your stakeholders are, the next step is to work through each stakeholder to **rate** their HEAT. Again, do this with a team if you can to remove your own biases and blind spots.

This step seems simple, and yes, you can probably belt through two dozen stakeholders in half an hour on your own. You'll have a full spreadsheet to show your boss and look productive. But you'll have learned nothing you didn't already know, and your gap will be no closer to closing.

So, treat this as a really valuable opportunity to discover something new, and build up some relationships in the process. Talk to multiple people before forming views. And for engagement, attitude and trigger, speak directly to the stakeholders themselves if you can. Doing so can increase both their engagement and attitude, so that's a bonus! **Coalitions form in consultation.**

Here's what a HEAT Sheet might look like after you've finished the rate step.

Stakeholder	Heft	Engagement	Attitude	Trigger/s
1	high	low	positive	Family-oriented
2	low	high	neutral	Budget-conscious
3	unknown	high	hostile	Election pending
4	unknown	unknown	unknown	Retires soon

Figure 14.2: HEAT Sheet rate step

CONTEMPLATE

This next step is vital. This is the risk assessment step, and if you skip it, you'll really need that tetanus shot!

In this step, you (and possibly your project team) want to **contemplate** every stakeholder individually. You're going to review their HEAT ratings and consider what each combination means for your project.

There are an infinite number of possible combinations. I've provided four examples in the table overleaf to illustrate the point.

Stakeholder	Heft	Engagement	Attitude	Trigger	Opportunity/Risk
1	high	low	positive	Family-oriented	Powerful ally waiting to happen – get them engaged, stat! Tell them how the project is good for families. Ask for their input, so they start taking ownership and want to help.
2	low	high	neutral	Budget-conscious	They're paying attention, but still haven't formed a view. Probe them for more information on why they're interested. What does the project mean for them? Why are they on the fence? Engaging is low risk because their influence is low, high reward because their high interest means we'll get rich feedback.

Stakeholder	Heft	Engagement	Attitude	Trigger	Opportunity/Risk
3	unknown	high	hostile	Big contract pending	Trouble waiting to happen. They really don't like us, and we don't know how much heft they have. Engage heavily until we work out what's wrong and how influential they are.
4	unknown	unknown	unknown	Retires soon	Amber flag. All of these unknowns mean we may have an ally or an enemy. Missing either can be a blow to our project, and until those unknowns become known, this is a risk we need to manage. Gently reach out to ask their views, and try to get a read on the unknowns.

Figure 14.3: HEAT Sheet contemplate step

CORRECT

Once you've completed these three steps (and ideally after you've also added the insights from doing a HEAT Map – see next chapter) you'll be in a strong position to see what actions to take next to **correct** matters.

The correcting step doesn't have to be exhaustive; not everyone has to be a cheerleader for your project. It's fine to have some low scores in there! Just make sure you thoroughly consider the implications so you know where your risks, and opportunities, are hiding.

RECAP

- HEAT Sheets are great ways to capture lots of information about stakeholders.

- Step 1 is to State them: identify each stakeholder, taking care not to miss people like I did with Simon. Best done with input from others.

- Step 2 is to Rate them: give them HEAT scores. Again, let others have a say. And remember, any "unknown" scores should be assumed to be bad until confirmed otherwise.

- Step 3 is to Contemplate: deliberate on what those HEAT scores are telling you. Where are there opportunities to increase support for your project? Where are there threats?

- Step 4 is to Correct: work out what to do with the insights from Step 3. Who needs some attention? Who needs to feel better listened to? Develop and execute a plan to get people on board as needed.

YOUR TURN

Flip back to the HEAT Sheet on the previous page. Assume you've been asked to reach out to all four of those stakeholders to improve each one's relationship to your project in some way.

1. Who would you start with? Why?

2. Who next? Then who's third? Then fourth? Why?

3. If your boss asked you to reach out first to the person you just put fourth in the last question, what would you do differently? Why?

15

The HEAT Map

The more you sweat, the luckier you get.

Ray Kroc, founder, McDonald's

The HEAT Map transforms the HEAT Sheet into a graphical form. Doing so reveals new insights. In synthesiser terms, this is a great edit activity.

PLOT

Either download our template or draw a diagram like the template in Figure 15.1 overleaf on a whiteboard. The whiteboard option is great for a workshop setting with your team, hint hint.

Now drop each stakeholder into their respective quadrant according to their **engagement** and **attitude**.

To denote **heft**, use lowercase, Title Case or UPPERCASE lettering (for low, medium, high).

Or you can use highlighters, stickers, spots and stripes, or anything else you have available. All that matters is that you know what it means, so make a key!

Figure 15.1: HEAT Map template

The HEAT Map in Figure 15.2 is populated by the mock data from Chapter 14. Notice how Stakeholder 4 is in UPPERCASE letters and in the Danger quadrant. But in the HEAT Sheet, they're ranked as having unknown heft, influence and interest.

So why have I mapped them as their worst options on all those scores? Because **you should always treat an unknown rating as "bad" until you determine otherwise**.

Bad = high heft, high engagement + low attitude.

(Pedant's note: high engagement isn't itself bad. It's only bad when it's combined with a low attitude). Taking this precautionary approach avoids Simons.

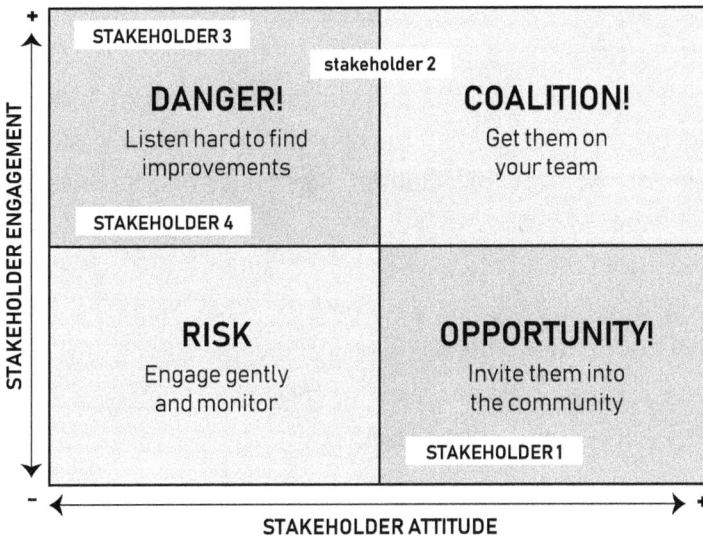

Figure 15.2: HEAT Map example

CONSIDER

Once you've put all of your stakeholders on the HEAT Map, stand back and **consider** the map as a whole. Here are some questions you can discuss with your colleagues to spark insight:

- What patterns can we see?
- What surprises us?
- Who might be influencing who?
- Where are the greatest opportunities to increase our project's support?

Meld these insights with what you learned in the HEAT Sheet, then set about correcting as in Sheet Step 4.

Now, you may be asking – didn't we just create two documents with the same information? Well, yes. And that's fine. In fact, it's better than fine, because each has different uses. The HEAT Map allows you to capture a lot of information graphically and easily shows the relativity between stakeholders. The HEAT Sheet allows a more analytical consideration.

When you show these tools to your coalition, you'll see that some will lean toward the HEAT Sheet, some the HEAT Map. That's because people's brains work differently. Generally, the big-picture thinkers will appreciate the HEAT Map, whereas the more detail-oriented thinkers will be drawn to the HEAT Sheet. Do what works.

RECAP

- HEAT Maps take the raw data of HEAT Sheets and put them into a visual format.

- This allows fresh insights that staring at a spreadsheet can miss.

- When mapping, treat all unknown HEAT rankings as their worst option until you establish otherwise. This will stop nasty surprises.

YOUR TURN

1. Turn back to the mock HEAT Map above, showing the four stakeholders. Come up with three insights from what you see there.

2. Do you think that those insights would have been easier or harder to pull out of the HEAT Sheet?

16

How to attract the right people to your side

People will forget what you said, people will forget what you did,
but people will never forget how you made them feel.

Maya Angelou

At the beginning of this Part, I told you my tale of accidental success forming my first coalition of support. I got lucky that time; we all get lucky, sometimes. But I'd prefer it if you didn't have to rely on luck. So in this chapter, I've collated methods drawn from my own and others' lives, underpinned by psychological research, that will help you deliberately and repeatedly attract the right people into your coalitions.

Resist the desire to go it alone. Embrace the need to bring people together. Remember, no matter how smart you are, no matter how qualified, you do not, can not, know everything, even about simple problems. Our world is too complex.

But knowledge, as they say, is power, so the more knowledge you have about a problem, the more likely you are to solve it.

These two opposing truths create a quandary! How do we get over this knowledge hurdle? By harnessing other people.

In this chapter we'll use HEAT as our framework for exploring tools to build coalitions.

BUT... PEOPLE ARE SCARY!

I want to acknowledge that **building relationships is a skill that can be daunting** for many of us. That can go double when you're new to the professional world.

If the mere thought of this chapter is giving you sweaty palms, that suggests it's worth you investing some time into your own development here. I say this because forming strong working relationships is vital to closing gaps; there's just no way around that.

But don't despair – forming strong *working* relationships doesn't mean being the life of the party! They're not the same at all. In fact, forming strong working relationships can be surprisingly easy; even office small talk makes a big contribution to people figuring out if they can trust you.[1]

Forming coalitions of support has a lot more to do with the three characteristics from Chapter 11 that underpin social license – credibility, legitimacy and trust. It's not like in school; nobody cares what you're wearing or how rich your parents are.

At work, people care about whether you're competent, honest, thoughtful, trustworthy, and whether what you're doing makes a difference.

If you think you'd benefit from some extra development effort to build your people skills, there are some truly excellent books out there. I recommend starting with the classics – *How to Win Friends and Influence People* by Dale Carnegie and *The 7 Habits of Highly Effective People* by Stephen Covey are the old favourites of millions, for a reason. Even reading summaries online will enhance your peopling skills no end.

Now, back to the matter at hand.

START WITH HEAT

To embark on a deliberate process of engagement, first you need to gather information. The best stakeholder information is their HEAT. Each element of HEAT will give you clues about how to proceed. Use the HEAT Sheet and HEAT Map tools from Chapters 14 and 15.

Use your stakeholders' Heft score to help identify who needs to be in your coalition. Coalitions don't necessarily need to be made up of the most powerful or influential people – far from it. While most projects might need a bit of that, they also need doers. Those with power are rarely those who will do most of the work! So a mix is vital.

Identify your stakeholders' Triggers to suggest the narratives that might connect with them to increase their Engagement or improve their Attitude, as required.

The remainder of this chapter will lay out some reliable methods for increasing Engagement, improving Attitude or both. This isn't a sequential process; forming relationships isn't that linear. Instead, you must use your judgement as to which tool/s to use, when and how.

Sound daunting? Practise. As with everything in this book, starting small helps you get good for cheap now, so that you've got skills to lean on when the stakes are higher later.

DEVELOP YOUR WEB OF RELATIONSHIPS BEFORE YOU NEED THEM

Every relationship teaches you something. Every introduction you make or insight you pass on adds to your credibility and value. So, for those reasons and many more, you should develop the habit of building up relationships everywhere and every time you can.

There is no such thing as an influential person who doesn't have a large network of positive relationships with people at all levels, in all sorts of situations. There is also no such thing as a useless contact.

While it's always possible to form a relationship "just in time" at the start of a project, you'll usually get better results if you've got a pre-existing relationship with the relevant people.

However, don't let lack of existing relationships slow you down – it can also be true that strong relationships are forged through joint projects, even "being in the trenches together". **Start where you're at now.**

Now, how do you form a relationship with someone? Well, many of the other steps in this chapter will help you do that. A relationship is really just a personal version of social license – it's not something you *do*, so much as it's a by-product of doing other things, well. And it is fostered by the same trifecta – credibility, legitimacy and above all, trust.

SPEND YOUR TIME SAVING THEIRS

Before reaching out to someone, do them the courtesy of putting a minute into working out what you're reaching out for. Maybe you need a question answered, maybe you're asking them to attend a meeting, review a document or share a social media post to their network. Whatever it is, be clear with yourself about the purpose of your outreach.

That doesn't mean cut to the chase. You might talk to them for an hour about all sorts of things. In fact, that can be its own point – just putting in the time to forge or maintain a relationship.

The five minutes you put into getting clear on why you're engaging will increase the quality of the engagement and decrease the amount of aimless time you waste in their day.

SOLVE A PROBLEM OF THEIRS

I can't stress this enough – **nobody cares why a project matters to you. They care why it matters to them.** So, in order to get someone into your coalition of support, you must tell them how what you're asking of them solves their problem. Don't know their problem? Check back to their trigger.

Let me illustrate by sharing a tale that's still irritating me. I'm selling my house, so each week, my agent rings me with an update. Annoyingly, he spends the whole call on what matters to *him*, not to me. Case in point, last week he told me he'd spoken to seven interested buyers – I was elated! But next breath, he says two had already dropped out and three more were on the fence. Ugh; excited to annoyed in a nanosecond.

Reflecting on the call later, I surmised that one of the metrics his bosses (power) probably measure him on is the number of interested parties he speaks to (success), whereas the only metric I care about is whether anyone is making an offer to buy (impact).

So telling me all about the calls he's had makes him feel like he's demonstrating value to me, but it leaves me feeling like he's wasted my time, and worse, gotten my hopes up for nothing. Guess who's looking for another agent...

So, before you speak to anyone about anything ever, I want you to stick these two points together – have a clear idea of what you're seeking *and* what's in it for them. Think that's nuts? Try it for a day and see how much more rapport you build.

ASK FOR THEIR INPUT

This tip is a doozy, yet I can't count the number of times I've witnessed it get skipped. One of the best methods to get buy-in while also ensuring your project actually solves problems is to **ask your stakeholders to help you design (or refine) your project**. There is no faster way to build trust than by throwing open the doors and handing over the reins.

It's a rare project that has no scope whatsoever for letting others shape it. If not its goals or budget, could they help shape the timetable? The milestones? The pilot?

Giving people the ability to "hold the pencil" – to set some of the terms of the project – helps them develop a sense of ownership, and that helps turn stakeholders into coalition members. Remember, the best thing that can ever happen to *your* project is for a coalition member to call it *theirs*.

RESOLVE THEIR BLIND BLACK BLOCKS

Recently I had a client who wanted my help with articulating the excellence of his company's program. I thought it would be easy, as I already knew their program was superb. But when he sent me the relevant material and shared his thoughts on what needed doing, I couldn't make heads nor tails of it. The problem wasn't clear to me, and thus, I wasn't sure what to do.

You know that feeling, right? You've been tasked with something that seems straightforward, but when you sit down to do it, you find yourself scratching your head and not knowing where to begin. Awful.

So, I rang the client to talk through the project a bit more. Then I realised why I couldn't see straight – my client was in a Blind Black Block.

Blind Black Block is a term I coined to denote a particularly sticky state of being:

- **Blind**, because the person in the state isn't consciously aware they're in it
- **Black**, because they lack clarity; they're in the dark
- **Block**, because they're stuck until they do something differently.

So, a Blind Black Block (BBB) is a state of being where someone knows they've got a problem to solve, but they don't really know what it is. More than simply being unclear, **someone inside a Blind Black Block isn't even clear about what they're unclear about**.

This makes it very difficult to get out. However, it also means that they'll be grateful to anyone who can throw them a lifeline.

You can train yourself to spot BBBs and then help people out of them. Spotting them is mostly a matter of learning to recognise the fuzzy, confused sense you get when you encounter a person, problem or project – the feeling that jumped from my client to me when he handed me the brief.

Pro tip: don't assume a feeling of fuzziness is because you're inexperienced or out of your depth. It may be a BBB!

Getting someone out of a BBB is pretty simple, because they're the ones that do the work. You're just the one who prompts them. All you need to do is ask them questions that will help them to find an island of certainty in a sea of question marks.

Some examples include:

- What are you trying to achieve? Who are you trying to please? What problem are you trying to solve?
- Where's the pain in this situation? What hurts?
- Who's asking for what? What's in the way of providing that?

- Which part of this problem is keeping you up at night? What is it about that part that really troubles you?
- How do you wish this situation would resolve itself?
- Have you felt/dealt with similar concerns to this before? If so, what did you do?

Notice any missing words in that list?

There are no "why" questions. Why?

I deliberately avoid asking why questions to BBB sufferers. Using what/where/how questions avoids triggering peoples' natural defence mechanisms.

Try it out for yourself. Imagine telling your boss about, say, a messy conversation you just had, and your boss asking you, "Why did you do that?" Does that question make you feel introspective or defensive? Most people will feel defensive.

You're trying to throw someone a lifeline here, not have them argue with you that they're not drowning.

RECAP

- Attracting people to your coalitions can be done with deliberateness.
- If the thought of stakeholder engagement makes you queasy, take heart.
- Forming professional relationships has more to do with credibility, legitimacy and trust than with popularity or entertainment value.

- The best framework for deliberative relationship building is HEAT.

- Heft can inform who to target for inclusion in your coalition. A mix of high and low heft is vital for getting work done.

- Triggers are the gateways to shifting peoples' engagement and attitudes.

- Many tools exist to build rapport. However there is no formula; humans are complex, and we must each hone our own judgement to decide the right tool for each engagement.

- Cultivate relationships widely; influential people always have networks that are both wide and deep.

- Don't waste people's time. Take the onus upon yourself to work out the purpose of your interactions before you have them. This shows respect and builds trust.

- Articulate why your project or request solves a problem of theirs. Nobody cares why it matters to you; they care why it matters to them.

- Asking people to input into your project in meaningful ways is a fast track to strong engagement and favourable attitudes. It breeds their sense of ownership, which can turn *your* project into *their* project.

- Learn to recognise and resolve Blind Black Blocks (BBB). People remember how you made them feel. If you can pull them out of a BBB they are more likely to think of you as someone helpful and wise and who makes them feel relief, clarity or hope.

YOUR TURN

1. Choose the tool from this chapter you feel the most attracted to or confident to use. Then go use it sometime today. Note how it goes, and what that teaches you for tomorrow.

2. Choose the tool that scares you or confuses you the most. Reflect on what about that tool puts you off. Be as honest with yourself as you can be.

3. Now, do a hypothetical exercise in your head. The scenario is this – you've just successfully used the tool for the first time. No tricks, no fluke, you just prepared yourself to use it, and then did it, and it worked. Now, reflect back and ask yourself, "what did I do that worked?"

WRAPPING UP PART 3

We've covered some serious ground in this part, and you've got a lot of work to do now.

Your effort is worth it – stakeholders really are your ticket to influence. If you can learn how to engage and channel the right people into your coalitions of support, then you really can achieve anything.

From today on I want you to start identifying what type of stakeholder you're talking to in each interaction you have. I want you to start assessing their heft, engagement, attitude and triggers.

I want you to put together your first HEAT Sheet and HEAT Map if you haven't already. Keep your eyes peeled for that fuzzy feeling of a BBB.

Then use this chapter's suite of engagement tools to start building up your social license!

We're halfway through the book now. Only two Parts to go – this is the pointy end of closing gaps.

In Part 4, I'll teach you how to go looking for problems. Because you can't fix what you can't see...

PART 4

PROBLEMS

Find solvable problems worth solving

If I had an hour to solve a problem,
I'd spend 55 minutes thinking about the problem
and five minutes thinking about solutions.

Albert Einstein

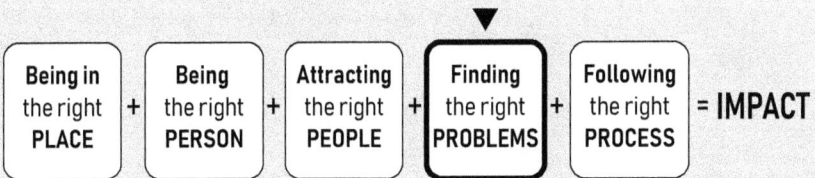

Being in		Being		Attracting		Finding		Following	
the right **PLACE**	+	the right **PERSON**	+	the right **PEOPLE**	+	the right **PROBLEMS**	+	the right **PROCESS**	= **IMPACT**

I started this book with the assumption that you want to close gaps. We close gaps by fixing problems. Can't fix what we can't see, so in this Part that's what you'll be learning – **the fourth P – finding the right Problems**.

Some problems are nicely contained, but the reality for most public servants is that even day-to-day problems have a way of tracing back up to big problems. This can be overwhelming.

So the trick isn't so much in finding a problem per se – they're everywhere. It's in finding the right chunk of a problem that's big enough to be meaningful, yet small enough to be manageable. In other words, **to find a solvable problem, worth solving**.

Now you might be asking "who gets to carve out their own problems to solve? I just get my work assigned to me." I get that.

When I talk about finding problems, I mean it in a couple of ways.

The first is that, within the envelope of whatever task you've been given, there's always going to be some scope for you to do things this way or that. This is that discretionary effort we spoke about in Chapter 8. Which way you use that effort will depend on what you understand the problem to be.

And second, while right now the work assigned to you may be specific – process this invoice, teach this lesson plan, inspect this dry cleaner – as you establish yourself as a sensible and trustworthy member of the team, you'll be given projects with greater and greater ambiguity. AKA, more scope for you to identify and tackle problems how you see fit.

DISRUPTION

There are great changes surging all around us – BLM, MeToo, renewable energy, electric cars, trans rights, internet of things, the gig economy... As a result, the world you hand to your grandkids will barely resemble the one being handed to you. Old ways of doing things are collapsing and being replaced with new ideas every day. These great changes – which I call **disruptions** – are neither intrinsically good nor bad. But you'd better believe that each one has winners and losers aplenty.

As a young person you may be so used to disruptions that you don't even recognise they're noteworthy – isn't that just the way the world is?

But ask anyone over 50 and they'll tell you the world used to be a bit more stable. Change happened more slowly, and most people's worlds were smaller and more predictable.

Why is disruption accelerating? What does it mean for you and your job? And how can you make sense of all this tumult to get the best outcomes for the people you serve?

The Australian Royal Commission into Natural Disaster Arrangements made this astute observation in its final report, "As the events of the 2019 and 2020 bushfire season show, **what was unprecedented is now our future.**" This statement could apply to so much happening in the world today.

Each disruption means new challenges for public servants. That's because the laws, policies and practices that exist now were all built in response to things *as they are*, or more often, *as they were*.

It's rare that any agency is built to manage things *as they will be*. To be fair, the past used to be a good predictor of the future. So building systems to cope with what history revealed to be the worst case was a sensible strategy.

But with the trend in global disruptions leading to ever-greater extremes for our economies, societies and the environment, **the past is no longer a good predictor of the future**. Now, public servants must act based not on past evidence, but on prediction. This is part of what we'll cover in coming chapters.

But before I go on, two warnings…

BEWARE OVER-REACH

I have a bad habit. My coach calls it Superwoman Syndrome – I try to fix everything I see, as quickly as possible, with little heed to my bandwidth or capability. This has led me to physical injuries, and more dangerously, to mental and emotional burnout.

As a passionate young public servant intent on closing gaps, you're vulnerable to Superwoman (or man) Syndrome. That's dangerous, and futile. Trying to do more than you're ready for is a good way to get crushed.

What we discuss in the next few chapters may tempt you to tackle everything, *right now.* **Please don't.**

The point of this part is to **progressively zoom in to a scale you can safely tackle at your current bandwidth and capability.** Over the course of your career, you'll scale up.

Remember, every giant world-shaking disruption is made up of millions of smaller problems. **Every problem that you solve helps.**

FEAR NOT

Living in this wild century, it's easy to feel scared by the scale of disruption happening around us. How many of you start your day by doomscrolling?

Despite all of that, **there is good reason to feel optimistic.**

A new and better future is within our reach. And you're part of the worldwide army helping us get there!

In 2020, futurists James Arbib and Tony Seba of RethinkX (www. rethinkx.com) published the extraordinary *Rethinking Humanity* report, arguing the case for hope. Here's a happy excerpt:

> With geographic expansion no longer possible, order of magnitude improvements in technological capabilities offer the only way to break through. This is exactly what we're seeing today... **As a result, climate change, inequality, and many of the other serious problems society faces today can be solved.**[1]

As a public servant, you're going to be part of navigating disruptions – first small ones, then bigger ones as you grow.

In this Part I'll let you know what's expected of you, introduce you to the biggest global disruptions, teach you how to predict disruptions before they arrive, show you how to trace them down to your own back yard, and finally guide you in how to carve out manageable problems to tackle.

17

People expect governments to manage disruptions

In the late '90s I encountered, for the first time in my life, a futurist. Til then I'd never even heard of such a thing. This person's job was literally to pontificate about what was coming.

I was gobsmacked! Here was I, cramming jam into donuts for minimum wage while cramming stats into my head for exams. And this bloke was making a good living by guessing the future! I decided I was in the wrong line of work.

Here's what I didn't have the wisdom to realise then. Any monkey can squish sugar paste into baked goods. But it takes skill and insight to look at the chaos of the world and see the patterns.

Those who can go further, to see the patterns *before* they resolve into a freight train coming right at you, are highly valued for good reason.

We know what citizens expect from their governments, because it's in the Public Sector Purpose from Chapter 1 – *to deliver what your jurisdiction needs to thrive*.

When it comes to disruptions, what your jurisdiction needs to thrive boils down to two very simple steps:

1. Maximise the good bits.
2. Minimise the bad bits.

We're going to add a step at the front – see it coming – because the sooner you can see a freight train coming, the more time you have to get out of the way.

So, the revised and slightly-more-formal-sounding list of what your constituents expect looks like this:

1. Foresee disruptions.
2. Maximise constituents' benefits.
3. Minimise constituents' costs.

I'm simplifying, but then, that's what I'm trying to do throughout this book! Even giant globe-sized hairy scary problems are still built out of lots of teeny little problems, and both big and small can be solved using the same fundamental processes.

Start on the teeny little ones, then gradually work your way up to the giant globe-sized hairy scary problems.

Let's start by unpacking those three steps.

1. FORESEE DISRUPTIONS

Citizens expect governments to foresee disruptions, because it's the way that governments can then minimise the bad and maximise the good.

Citizens expect governments to have foresight whether it's reasonable or not. Yes, even (especially) when the world is changing rapidly.

The good news is that, while individual changes are unpredictable, it's still possible to spot the patterns quickly and thus, have warning – see Chapter 21.

You might think that your agency will be fine to respond as disruptions come up. But the truth is, if all you do is respond, then not only are you unlikely to minimise constituents' costs or maximise their benefits, but you're also likely to piss off everyone in the process.

As I write this, large chunks of the east coast of Australia are under water. There's a very angry chorus of voters who are demanding to know why they were left so unprepared, and what's going to be done to prevent it happening again. Federal, state and even local governments are being flayed for failing to foresee.

Your bosses are thinking hard about how to predict the future. You have the ability to help them by seeing the view from the ground, talking to different people from them, and synthesising clues that your bosses might miss from way up there.

2. MAXIMISE CONSTITUENTS' BENEFITS

Once governments see stuff coming, citizens expect them to seize the benefits. After all, if it's a disruption caused by humans (as opposed to, say, a natural disaster), it's probably happening because there's a lot of benefits. Maybe not benefits to you or me, but to somebody.

For instance, back in 2019 while at the Clean Energy Council, I had a ringside seat to the debate raging about how to manage Australia's coal export market. This is no small matter; at the time,

Australia was the world's largest coal exporter (at the time of writing, we still are, accounting for a whopping 40 per cent of global exports, more than twice that of runner-up Indonesia). Of course, in our increasingly carbon-constrained world, the commodity that was once the backbone of Australia's export trade is now a growing risk.

So it should come as no surprise that a lot of smart public servants in Australia's governments are considering how to pivot to new exportable fuels like hydrogen, powered by our abundant wind and solar resources.

Australia could be a global renewable energy powerhouse in the 21st century and beyond, if it moves swiftly. To do so, governments across the country will need to foresee the disruption, work hard to maximise the possible benefits, and then...

3. MINIMISE CONSTITUENTS' COSTS

The final thing citizens expect governments to do here is minimise the likelihood that they suffer damage as disruptions go about rearranging things. As well as the obvious damage caused by losing the old, there's also the possibility of damage from failing to gain the new.

I doubt I'll shock you by pointing out that minimising costs is tricky. Disruptions have winners and losers, so one group's cost will likely be the source of another group's benefit.

Think about the arrival of DVDs, and then Blu-ray and then high-speed internet, cheap online storage and Netflix. Suddenly, our capacity to transport, store and retrieve high-quality data exploded. From movies to music to files, everyone got access to a lot more storage in a lot less space.

But if you were a VCR manufacturer, well, sucks to be you. And for older people, the change in technology has left their earlier home recordings and movie collections in an obsolete format. Good luck getting your VCR repaired in 2030.

It's often not fair, helpful or indeed even possible to completely prevent your citizens suffering costs from disruption. Some costs are unavoidable. Some costs serve to hasten an inevitable transition. Some costs are the price we pay for much larger benefits.

In practice, minimising costs and maximising benefits tend to be two sides of the same coin. The kind of interventions that citizens expect might include:

- warning of impending disruption
- identification of the specifics of the disruption, including who's likely to win and lose
- preventing, lessening or slowing down the disruption, perhaps through legislative blocking, inquiries or lockdowns
- conversely, accelerating, steering or leaning into the disruption, perhaps through subsidies, legislated targets or education campaigns
- shielding the ones who stand to lose out through things like buy-backs, job support, assistance to buy new equipment or tax breaks
- redistributing private sector windfalls to offset public losses through tariffs, resource taxes or levies.

BEING THE JUDGE

Given all of this, the best way for governments to "deliver what their jurisdiction needs" is to see disruptions coming, calmly and equitably assess the likely costs and benefits, use the Public Sector Principles to exercise their good judgement as to the most equitable course of action, then... get on with it. These actions all build up those golden characteristics of capability, legitimacy and trust, which grant you social license.

CASE STUDY: UBER

Disruptions pose critical questions for public servants. It'll be your job to both ask and answer them, even on the relatively small problems you're probably working on now.

To illustrate my point, here's an example that pretty much everyone will be familiar with. It's still working its way through our global system. Let's examine the rise of ride-sharing services such as Uber.[1]

Here are just a few of the public policy questions triggered by Uber's rise:

- Are Uber trips replacing private car use (reducing air pollution – good) or replacing public transport use (increasing air pollution – bad)?

- Do public transport agencies need to put on fewer buses/ trams/ferries/trains as people eschew mass transport, or more as people sell their cars?

- With thousands of taxi drivers who bought expensive taxi licences having now lost most of their value, what impact will that have on the pension system?

- What's the impact on government revenue from de-valued taxi licences?

- Are passengers more or less safe now that we're moving from a government controlled taxi-licencing model to private contracts?

- Will citizens' cardiovascular fitness increase or decrease due to ride-sharing?

Ask yourself now, what does Uber's rise mean for your agency's area of interest? I'm willing to bet that no matter how little your work has to do with transportation, if you think about it for a minute you'll find a connection.

SOMEBODY ELSE'S PROBLEM

I started this chapter with a quote from Terry Pratchett and I'm going to finish it with one from Douglas Adams. Some of the best truths, as they say, come from fiction.

In *Life, the Universe, and Everything*, book three of the incomparable *Hitchhiker's Guide to the Galaxy* series, a spaceship is cloaked in an "SEP (somebody else's problem) field" while parked in the middle of a cricket pitch. By using an SEP field, the ship becomes not so much invisible as wilfully ignored. A UFO in the middle of their match is too hard for spectators to comprehend, so they ignore it in the hope it will go away.

Somebody in your agency has probably said, "Just leave it for the market to work this out." Or perhaps, "We'll take a wait and see approach." In other words, make it somebody else's problem, even if "somebody else" is just us, later. That's avoidance, and it runs contrary to the Public Sector Principles. Don't accept it (if you have a choice).

Governments can't minimise constituents' costs or maximise benefits if they're sitting on the sidelines refusing to look at the spaceship. It might not be written into your agency's legislation to stare at spaceships, but I guarantee you that your citizens expect you to stare and respond – whether that's fair on your agency or not. **Because "somebody else" is you.**

PUBLIC SECTOR PURPOSE

To deliver what your jurisdiction needs to thrive.

PUBLIC SECTOR PRINCIPLES

1. Commitment to jurisdiction
2. Integrity and ethical conduct
3. Fairness and impartiality
4. Accountability
5. Human rights
6. Leadership
7. Effectiveness

RECAP

- Citizens expect governments to foresee risks, shield people from the harms and position society to reap the benefits.

- Whether that's the legislated purpose of your agency or not, it's what you'll get judged for in the court of public opinion.

- The pace of change is accelerating. So the world is changing, and it's changing faster than before. This isn't a coincidence.

- We used to be able to set public policy based on hindsight, but the past is no longer a good enough predictor of the future. So while hindsight will continue to give us wisdom, foresight is now more necessary than ever to illuminate that which hindsight has never seen.

- Minimising harm to constituents is tricky. Some harm serves a purpose. Some harm is unavoidable.

- Government's job will always be to think deeply about these matters. Citizens often don't have access to the information, analytics or other resources necessary to do such thinking themselves. That's what they pay you for.

- Every disruption has opportunity woven through the harm. Citizens expect governments to seize those opportunities and use those gains to offset losses elsewhere.

- It's government's job to make these judgement calls in the national interest, then to communicate them. Responding effectively to disruption isn't "somebody else's problem", it's yours.

YOUR TURN

1. Choose a recent topic from the news where a government entity (governing party, opposition, department, council, whatever) has really annoyed you. Consider it through the lens of this chapter to unpack your annoyance.

2. Did they fail to foresee the problem?

3. Did they miss a golden opportunity?

4. Did they leave a group of people hanging who didn't deserve it?

5. What Public Sector Principles were violated?

6. Consider who should've been involved but wasn't. Perhaps who was involved but shouldn't have been?

7. Think about what you'd have done differently. Then ask, why that? What talents or preferences of yours are showing through in your answers?

18

The mega-trends driving disruption

The farther backward you can look,
the farther forward you are likely to see.

Winston Churchill, WWII British Prime Minister

You know those moments when you realise you've put your foot in your mouth? They usually come about because you were missing a piece of context. That happened to me one day with a colleague, and I still cringe a little thinking about it now.

It all started when I bounced into a meeting room where a few people were already waiting. The room seemed tense, so I thought I'd have a go at breaking the ice. I'd just gotten a funny email from my mum and so I regaled the room with the tale. Mum this, Mum that.

I wasn't getting the kind of response I expected though; in fact, one lady looked positively crestfallen, and the two blokes in the room looked more awkward by the minute.

I slowly wound down, then asked the lady how her day was going. Her response – "My mum just died. I'm waiting for <boss> to arrive so I can tell her I'm leaving early to go help my dad."

Thud.

I'd inadvertently made a bad situation worse by not understanding the context.

In this chapter and the next, I'm going to give you a crash course in understanding the global, multi-decade (and even multi-century) trends that form the context in which you operate. I'm doing this because in order to close gaps, you must understand how they formed and understand the larger forces at play around you.

Think back to Chapter 6 and the ESE Model – economy as a subset of society as a subset of environment. When we think about the global system you (and I, and everyone else) are operating within, ESE is the lens we need.

So far in this book I've taken you on journeys into economics, philosophy, political science and psychology. Now it's time for a bit of history.

HOW IT STARTED

Human technology throughout most of the last millennium was fairly stable. Feudal systems saw peasants tilling fields and hand-weaving fabrics, making the various goods necessary to sustain life largely by hand.

Then along came the steam engine, and everything changed. The impact of the steam engine can't be overstated, because it ushered in what we now call the Industrial Revolution.

All of a sudden in the mid-18th century, we humans worked out how to build machines that could do the work for us, at a scale previously unimagined. A skilled weaver could make a yard of dress fabric in a day; an unskilled machine operator could make 1,000 yards. A skilled potter could make a dozen plates a day; an unskilled pottery mill worker could make 500.

For the first time, GDP (gross domestic product) started climbing (though the idea of GDP didn't yet exist). Until that point, most countries' economies had been largely stable. In the decades following the start of industrialisation, the previously low standards of living experienced by the vast majority of the Western world started rapidly climbing, as hitherto unreachable luxuries became affordable.

The global economy at the start of the industrial revolution was worth about $130 billion in today's dollars. (That's Australia's GDP now.) The global economy today is worth around $80 trillion. That's more than a five-hundredfold increase!

Meanwhile, the human population has exploded. The population in 1750 was only 650 million people, only around triple that of a thousand years earlier. Today, it's nearly 8 billion – that's an increase times 10 in just 250 years.

And sadly, since industrialisation, the planet has lost around 600 known species of plants and animals. Worse, there are a staggering 1 million that are currently under threat. That's over 1,600 times as many as we've already lost.

All of our economic growth has brought forth the kind of comfort, safety and capability that people even a century ago would call outright magic. We developed and then rolled out a vaccine for a global pandemic in less than 18 months; we've lifted billions out of poverty, and we're now on the brink of becoming an interplanetary species!

And yet, the cost of our advancement is placing our home planet in jeopardy. Looking at these three groups of stats together, we see that even though our population has only increased tenfold, both the economic output per person and the environmental destruction per person has skyrocketed.

How did that happen?

Humanity's ability to damage our outermost sphere has grown exponentially, largely **because we didn't design our growth to be costless**. We didn't think we needed to! Well, now we know better.

HOW IT'S GOING

For 60 years, a growing chorus of scientists, futurists and economists have been warning us that a great global disruption is coming. We stand on the shoulders of these giants, these key voices, so let's take a minute to listen.

Way back in 1962, Rachel Carson wrote a seminal book called *Silent Spring*. It kick-started the modern environment movement. In it, Carson explored how the use of insecticides to control mosquitoes and other nuisance insects was disrupting the whole food chain. This chemical disruption led to all sorts of weird and unexpected impacts, including loss of bird life (hence the book's title). These problems are still with us – have you noticed that there aren't as many butterflies now as when you were a kid?

In 1972, the Club of Rome commissioned a report that became another keystone book, *Limits to Growth* – the first mainstream book to point to global patterns of resource overuse.

More recently, we have examples such as Paul Gilding's 2011 book, *The Great Disruption*, which takes the idea underpinning *Limits to Growth* and folds in the more recent impacts of technology.

Going even further into the disruption, while also, refreshingly, examining the opportunities presented by 21st-century technological breakthroughs, in 2020 RethinkX released its groundbreaking *Rethinking Humanity* report, which I quoted from at the start of this Part. In *Rethinking Humanity*, RethinkX makes some bold predictions – for instance, that there will be no livestock industry in 30 years.[1] Can you imagine a world without cattle?

Hearing all of this, it's understandable if you feel like everything is going down the toilet – I certainly have that thought from time to time! You may have even grown up with a sense of foreboding, wondering if you'd have a future to live into.

But don't despair, because for all the stuff that's going wrong, there are so many signs that the harms that have accompanied our steady human progress are now being designed out of the system, and quickly. And it seems that COVID may even have helped: 75 per cent of consumers now have higher expectations on businesses, after seeing what dramatic shifts were possible during the pandemic.[2]

In the next chapter we'll look at some global disruptions that signal seismic cracks in the status quo.

Of course, it remains to be seen whether these global disruptions will avert disaster and who will get hurt along the way. The good news is, those are questions you'll be part of answering.

RECAP

- The modern era really only started with industrialisation.
- In less than 300 years, humanity's size and scale have exploded.
- There have been unimaginable improvements in every aspect of human life.
- However, the system that sprang up to grant this improvement wasn't designed to support us at this scale, and so the costs of this growth are reaching our planet's limits.
- Change is necessary, and it's happening.
- Public policy professionals such as you are part of shaping those changes.

YOUR TURN

1. Name five things that have gotten better since you were a kid. They may be local to you, global or anything in between. (This practice is one I use often to stave off feelings of anxiety or despair at the state of the world – a common peril for gap-closers.)

2. List five things that made you happy today. Perhaps:

   - your significant other or best friend did something to show you they care
   - something has gone your way lately
   - your boss or someone else taught you something new and insightful
   - you felt proud of your job
   - something happened to indicate you're on the right track.

19

A whistle-stop tour of the most relevant global disruptions

"Look again at that dot. That's here. That's home. That's us. On it everyone you love, everyone you know, everyone you ever heard of, every human being who ever was, lived out their lives. The aggregate of our joy and suffering, thousands of confident religions, ideologies, and economic doctrines, every hunter and forager, every hero and coward, every creator and destroyer of civilizations, every king and peasant, every young couple in love, every mother and father, hopeful child, inventor and explorer, every teacher of morals, every corrupt politician, every "superstar", every "supreme leader", every saint and sinner in the history of our species lived there – on a mote of dust suspended in a sunbeam."

– Carl Sagan, 1934–1996

You are here

Figure 19.1: You are here

When I was 11, I had a poster hanging in my room. Okay, I had loads, and most of them involved Joey McIntyre from New Kids on the Block.

But this particular poster was of space, with a beam of sunlight cutting through it. Within the sunbeam, a tiny blue dot. An arrow pointed to the dot, accompanied by the simple message "You are here".

My mum tells me that from the day that poster went up, I saw the world differently. I paid attention to what was happening, no matter where it was. Because what happened somewhere else, all of a sudden, mattered a great deal to one scrawny pre-teen in her NKOTB-plastered room in Texarkana, Texas, USA.

That poster is reproduced here, with the incomparably beautiful words of the late, great Dr Carl Sagan, astronomer and philosopher.

Dr Sagan had the honour of introducing this image to the world; one final loving glimpse of home by the *Voyager 1* spacecraft as it hurtled out of our solar system on Valentine's Day 1990. *Voyager* was, and is, the furthest that humanity has flung itself into our universe. The iconic "pale blue dot" image conveys what Dr Sagan understood, that so many of us struggle to – **we are all connected, for better and worse**.

Public servants will both push and be pulled by global disruptions. The ripples from each of the disruptions in this Part and many more are heading your way. And as sure as night follows day, there are both costs and benefits that your citizens are relying on you to manage on their behalf.

With that humbling thought in mind, in this chapter we're going to explore five global disruptions that are already changing the world, and have a long way to run yet. This is by no means a comprehensive list of global disruptions! But I've chosen these five because they're the most likely to be relevant to the wide audience of this book.

DISRUPTION 1: Dematerialising

What it is

The combination of gene sequencing, supercomputing and 3D printing allows humanity to once again transform manufacturing.[1] The Industrial Revolution was largely a revolution in manufacturing efficiency.

Two big gains were in *economies of scale* and *industrial forming* – think smelters, machines and moulds cranking out thousands of identical pieces in giant factories. No more handmade, no more bespoke, just mass-production.

But this is changing.

Gene sequencing gives humanity the ability to understand how all living things function. Supercomputing enables humanity to design ever-more-complex and tailored solutions. And 3D printing enables us to build whatever we can design, in small batches, on demand.

Combine the three, and we are seeing the beginnings of a global move toward *dematerialisation* – the ability to produce customised products to meet targeted needs. From shoes custom printed for your feet,[2] to microorganisms bred to eat waste plastic,[3] to lab-grown meat that doesn't raise your cholesterol,[4] the possibilities for transforming what and how we consume will soon be beyond today's imagination.

Why it's important

This bespoke approach to manufacturing largely eliminates manufacturing waste. This is great news for a planet already groaning under the strain of resource depletion and pollution.

The implications for reduced waste are mostly positive, but as we discussed above, every change brings both winners and losers. Job losses in resource extraction and refining will be significant, as will losses in transport logistics and manufacturing. Sectors that rely on waste streams will suffer, as will sectors that rely on the fast through-put of low-value consumer goods.

What might dematerialisation mean for your agency?

DISRUPTION 2: Automation

What it is

Automation is coming through technological advances in two areas. The first is software, in the form of artificial intelligence or AI (accelerated by supercomputing). The second is hardware, in the form of ever-more sophisticated robotics (accelerated both by AI and 3D printing).[5]

Automation is nothing new in manufacturing, though of course it's continuing to reach ever-higher penetration as costs plummet. But we're just starting to see it in sectors as far flung as medicine, transportation, counselling and finance.

For instance, hedge funds are now training artificial intelligence to watch videos of presentations by company executives.[6] The AI is able to detect whether those executives are telling the truth, whether they believe in the strategies and products they're pitching. These hedge funds are using those insights to make million-dollar investment decisions without employing fleets of human analysts. The savings result in better returns than human-powered funds as a result.

You might think this sounds like science fiction. Robots can't predict the future – life is not a Tom Cruise movie.

But as *Rethinking Humanity* states:

Technology disruptions are not linear progressions and they do not take decades to play out. They may appear to start slowly, but **they move exponentially as they trigger power-ful feedback mechanisms that drive extremely rapid change**. The impacts of which can ripple it out across not just the economy, but society itself.[7]

Why it's important

Automation increases production efficiency and reduces hazards for workers previously exposed to harsh conditions or toxic chemicals.

It will revolutionise the way we grapple with the problems facing our jurisdictions. The possibility to increase your agency's reach is huge.

If you're curious, go to your preferred search engine and put the following phrase in: "how automation is changing <insert your agency or job's area of concern, for example, child protection/HR/education>".

However, automation will also upturn the traditional way many of your citizens provide for themselves – aka, their jobs. Australia and much of the Western world saw wholesale layoffs in manufacturing through the '80s and '90s caused by the offshoring of production to countries with lower wages and safety standards. These layoffs ushered in a lost generation of young people, especially men, and led to widespread social corrosion.[8] The same pattern is emerging across the globe, as cheap labour is replaced by robots and AI.

The implications for government agencies are extensive. Schooling will need to change, with soft skills such as resilience and adaptability being elevated to the same importance as any technical skill. Retraining and mental health support will need to be available for affected workers. Taxation models that relied on payroll and consumption taxes will need to be overhauled.

What might automation mean for your agency?

DISRUPTION 3: Decentralisation

What it is

Only 20 years ago, if you lived in London and wanted to plan a trip to New York, you'd need to buy a Lonely Planet guidebook. Now, you jump on to the net, where you can walk virtually down each street and read people's reviews of each shop.

And 20 years ago, if you wanted electricity, you rang your (monopoly) utility provider to set up an account and were offered a choice of perhaps two tariffs. Today, you can choose from dozens of providers with different tariffs, or better yet, install solar and generate electricity yourself.

In short, 20 years ago when you wanted news, food, movies, personal loans, power tools or a myriad of other goods and services, they were provided to you by only a limited number of sources, in a way that suited the sellers more than the buyers.

Today, thanks mostly to the power of the internet and mobile phones, people – as consumers, citizens, voters, creators – can share information more broadly than ever before, self-organise around causes, find "alternative facts" and bypass traditional means of distribution.[9]

From the sharing economy to standalone power systems to citizen juries – coupled with the other big disruptions we discuss here – decentralisation will continue to redraw the boundaries of most human endeavours.

Why it's important

Governments used to have "pinch points" where control could be applied. For instance, when there were only two newspapers in town, getting your message to the public was pretty straightforward.

Or when students only had access to library books, then steering their learning journey was more a matter of getting them to read than preventing them from reading who-knows-what on the internet.

As the decentralisation of information and communication has changed the world around us, governments no longer have the same degree of visibility or influence they once did.

Yet simultaneously, citizens' expectations have increased – information must now be provided in multiple languages, through multiple formats, on multiple platforms, in real time and in a user-focused way.

In the next 20 years, we'll see the emergence of citizen-led patrolling of the world, too – already, citizens are reporting potholes,[10] pollution[11] and perpetrators[12] on public apps.

You can expect that whatever your agency does, you'll need to open your doors to your data, and allow the public to participate in data generation, decision-making and other processes that were once done behind closed doors by experts.

What else might decentralisation mean for your agency?

DISRUPTION 4: Climate change

What is it

We won't labour this one – as a young person, the odds are that you know far more about climate change than you want to. I know I'm exhausted at the frequency with which it needs to be discussed.

But it would be weird to discuss global disruptions without mentioning it. The key point I'll make here is that pretty soon, there will be no jurisdiction untouched by the effects of climate change.[13] Whether your agency considers itself to be "frontline" or not – it is. If your agency isn't grappling with the impacts (or at least, preparing to grapple) then you will be soon.

Why it's important

The pressure that climate change will exert on all human and natural systems can't be overstated. As a public servant, you'll not only be expected to facilitate your jurisdiction's management of this greatest of disruptions – you personally will also, in time, be in a position to influence how much your jurisdiction does to avert the worst.

One purpose of this book is to help you go as far as you want, as fast as you want – and no problem will need more energy applied to solving it than climate change. So whether you stay on the front line or head up into leadership, climate change will define much of what you do in your career.

What does climate change mean for your agency? Consider that question for yourself, and look at it from these angles:

- **Mitigation** – that's the "minimising costs" discussion from earlier.
- **Drawdown** – the wondrous idea of seeking ways to reverse climate change by drawing carbon out of the atmosphere. If you're working in agriculture, this is the most, ahem, fertile area for drawdown potential.
- **Transformation** – this is the "maximise benefits" discussion. What advantages can be seized for your jurisdiction during this big upheaval?

DISRUPTION 5: Changing capitalism

What is it

Capitalism – the dominant economic philosophy of the last 250 years – has brought humanity untold wealth, comfort and development. I'm writing this book on my fast computer with its rainbow-illuminated keyboard, in my climate-controlled home office, saving my work in real-time to the cloud. I stream music through my wireless head-phones and my toe is tapping within my custom-moulded ergonomic shoes and moisture-wicking socks. I'm surrounded, in short, by countless examples of the way that capitalism has brought me comfort and aided my creative journey.

However, for reasons spelled out in this Part already, it's simultaneously true that capitalism as it's been delivered so far has brought many parts of our planet to the point of collapse. In fact, a global survey of over 30,000 respondents found that 56% believe that "capitalism as it exists today does more harm than good".[14]

Put into extremely simplified terms, capitalism as it's been done for the last 250-odd years has fuelled growth through resource extraction, without limits, and without regard to system health as a whole.

This was fine when we were only a few billion people, and when our technological capacity was still relatively modest. But in the latter half of the 20th century, both our numbers and our power grew exponentially. That put us on a collision course with the outermost sphere, and that's a fight we can't win.

Thankfully, **a new and improved form of capitalism is emerging**. It has many names, but the one I prefer is *regenerative capitalism.*

Regenerative capitalism recognises that humanity's existence is bound by our planetary context, that due to our increased scale we're all tied together now, and that the only way to sustain our current (and rising) standard of living is to reimagine the way that our global economy works.[15]

We're seeing regenerative capitalism emerging in all sorts of ways. The sharing economy. Social enterprises. Ethical investing. Divestment campaigns. Workers' capital.

In fact, if you look at the other disruptions explored in this chapter, you'll see how they each feed into, and off of, this overhaul of capitalism.

Two emerging international trends that epitomise the spirit of regenerative capitalism are *circular economy* and *just transition*.

Circular economy refers to the redesign of manufacturing and recycling to "close the loop" and remove the concept of waste from our economy. This closely overlaps disruption 1: dematerialisation.

Just transition is an umbrella movement covering the wide spectrum of labour force issues brought about by all of these disruptions. Starting as a way to advocate for the fossil fuel industry workers left stranded by the rise of renewable energy, the movement has grown to encapsulate most of the human issues caused by "old capitalism".

While the fundamentals of capitalism such as free enterprise and incentives for innovation aren't changing, they're growing new boundaries that better safeguard our shared health. This is exactly the kind of iteration and improvement that we should expect from a species clever enough to colonise Mars (and invent the Mars Bar).

Why it's important

If we don't redefine the parts of capitalism that have outlived their usefulness, the costs will rapidly outstrip our capacity to pay them.

However, if we can successfully harness its power in service of a more holistic set of goals, then by the time we're old, humanity may have entered a golden era.

This is exactly the kind of "minimise costs, maximise benefits" scenario that our forebears created governments to manage!

Redefining the rules of the economic sphere won't be smooth, nor will the process be uncontested. "Old capitalism" structures abound – for instance, the corporations' responsibility to shareholders discussed in Chapter 1, enshrined in most country's legal frameworks. That's hard to rewrite, though of course not impossible.

Governments around the world have started enshrining triple bottom line accounting into their cost-benefit analyses. Under the banner of a federal circular economy framework, three Australian states have now launched ambitious circular economy plans (Victoria, South Australia and Tasmania, as of January 2022).

And the WA Government is leading the way on Just Transitions for some of its traditional coal-mining regions. Here's an excerpt from their *Collie Just Transition Plan*[16] that I honestly couldn't have written any better to make my point:

> Collie's Just Transition Working Group (JTWG) includes members from across industry, government and community to ensure affected people are considered by decision-makers and that early action towards a Just Transition can **minimise the negative impacts and maximise positive opportunities**.

How might the shift to regenerative capitalism make your job easier? Harder?

RECAP

- Human society has expanded to the scale that we're now all connected.
- As human growth outstrips the planet's carrying capacity, we're seeing more global disruptions.
- The top five most likely to affect broad swathes of the Australian public sector are dematerialisation, automation, decentralisation, climate change and changing capitalism.

- Each of these disruptions represents risks and opportunities for your jurisdiction and your agency.

- The job of all public servants is to have an eye to these mega-issues so that they can inform your on-the-ground work.

YOUR TURN

Look back on the five disruptions mentioned in this chapter and answer the following questions for each disruption:

1. How might this global disruption impact my current role and my agency's remit?

2. What light can this disruption shed on the issues within my proximity?

20

Global disruptions affect local lives

Toe bone connected to the foot bone,
foot bone connected to the heel bone…

'Dem Bones', gospel song

In June 2021, a whopping great wind-storm blew through the Dandenong Ranges, on the outskirts of Melbourne. This is where I hang my hat.

The Dandenongs are renowned for being heavily forested – we have suburbs called Ferntree Gully and Tremont (tree mountain). Towering gum trees, stretching 50 metres up to the sky, frame every view.

So when 100km/hour winds ripped through, coming from a direction that we rarely experience, it wreaked havoc. 25,000 huge trees were ripped from the ground. Their roots, so well established for the prevailing wind direction, were unprepared and unable to hold them up as they were buffeted on their weak sides.

Our local Council, Yarra Ranges Shire, was inundated with calls from residents with fallen or failing trees on Council land. I was one of them – three gums on our front boundary had lifted but not fallen, leaning precariously toward surrounding houses and making them disasters waiting to happen.

To my Council's enormous credit, they scrambled resources to help at a spectacular speed during a pandemic. I will be forever grateful to Glenn and the rest of the Council's tree team for their sterling efforts – they deserve this shout-out.

Now, why did that wind-storm hit, and so severely? Well, it's hard to slate any natural disaster to climate change but science tells us that such severe weather events will be more common.

Glenn and his team can't tackle climate change. But they can and do tackle the consequences. Many months later, they're still helping residents rebuild their lives after the storm. No doubt by the time this storm is cleaned up, it'll be the next one. Or a bushfire. Or the next wave of Covid, or whatever else comes along.

Global issues lead to local problems – that's why you need to learn to recognise global issues.

Now it's time to show you a straightforward method to work out how those global issues relate to your area of influence.

KEVIN BACON

The easiest way I know to connect our everyday work to global disruptions is with a **Causation Map**. Think about it like *Six Degrees of Kevin Bacon*.[1]

It can sometimes be hard to see all the way from a big global issue right down to your day-to-day work, so it helps to break it down into steps. I also find it helps to start with what you know best – your own tasks.

That's why we start our Causation Map by thinking about an issue we deal with regularly. Then all we have to do is think about what might be driving that, just one level up. That's usually easy enough.

Then we go another level up, which might be where it starts getting a bit trickier, and you might need to do a bit of thinking or asking other people. But still doable, right?

Then the next step up – again, maybe some thinking, asking, research. And on you go, just one step at a time, until you get up to a level where you can see a big disruption.

Here's an example:

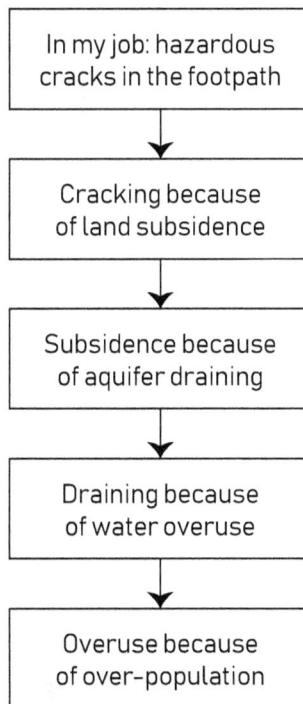

```
┌─────────────────────────┐
│ In my job: hazardous    │
│ cracks in the footpath  │
└─────────────────────────┘
            │
            ▼
┌─────────────────────────┐
│ Cracking because        │
│ of land subsidence      │
└─────────────────────────┘
            │
            ▼
┌─────────────────────────┐
│ Subsidence because      │
│ of aquifer draining     │
└─────────────────────────┘
            │
            ▼
┌─────────────────────────┐
│ Draining because        │
│ of water overuse        │
└─────────────────────────┘
            │
            ▼
┌─────────────────────────┐
│ Overuse because         │
│ of over-population      │
└─────────────────────────┘
```

Figure 20.1: Causation Map

If you're finding this a bit of a challenge, try drawing the map in reverse – start with the global challenge and trace it down to your job.

Now, perhaps you're wondering, why bother? I mean, if you're getting work orders to go fix cracks in the pavement, what use is it to know that this might be driven by over-population? Glad you asked.

Every time you work through a Causation Map, you're training your brain to see connections more rapidly. This is a form of strategic thinking, and it'll make you better at far more than just doing Causation Maps.

Second, it's often easier to spot big trends than little ones, because other people are busy looking for them. In the next chapter I'm going to recommend a bunch of "voices" to listen to which will help you see big disruptions coming. So by pairing those early warning systems with your newly trained connection-forming brain, you'll see problems near you much more easily.

Thirdly, when you build up the habit of doing Causation Maps (either on paper or in your head), you'll start noticing patterns that you may not otherwise have seen. When you notice, for instance, cracks in the pavement in a particular suburb are increasing at the same time as water leaks, and both might be connected to subsidence, then maybe instead of dealing with the cracks, you can make the case for dealing with the subsidence that's coming from, say, a nearby mine or major construction. One solution that could tackle lots of problems.

Issues dealt with in isolation become like a game of Whack-A-Mole. But smart public servants train themselves to look for patterns, and use those patterns to identify the best place to apply their energy to get maximum bang for buck. Kevin Bacon would approve.

RECAP

- Big problems break down into lots of little problems.

- Little problems are very often symptoms of much bigger problems.

- It's possible to find the threads that link big and little problems.

- Causation Maps are a great method to do that.

- Training your brain to see these links will make you a better strategic thinker.

- Practising this habit can enable you to detect patterns in little problems that can uncover shared root causes, meaning that government resources can be applied to tackle greater bang-for-buck problems.

YOUR TURN

1. Do a Causation Map! Choose a problem you work on daily and see what global trend you can connect it to.

2. Choose another global trend and do this Causation Map in reverse – trace it down to a problem you face.

21

How to see disruptions coming

Foresight is not about predicting the future,
it's about minimizing surprises.

Karl Schroeder, futurist

In Netflix's *The Queen's Gambit*, we meet Beth, a fictional chess savant who can visualise whole games in her head. She becomes one of the best in the world, because she can foresee risks and calmly work out how to avoid them, all while methodically tying her opponents in knots.

Now it's time to give you three tools to let you foresee disruptions that are coming toward your jurisdiction or your sector. In Part 5, I'll show you how to avoid them, while tying your opponents – problems – up in knots.

1. BORROW OTHER PEOPLE'S BRAINS

Predicting the future may not be something you're very good at (yet). But a lot of smart cookies are out in the world doing all sorts of clever things. Many of them are kind enough to pop their ponderings down on websites, podcasts and email blasts.

Here is a list of some of the best future-scanners and innovation-makers; sign up to their mailing lists, follow them on socials and generally soak up their wisdom.

This list isn't comprehensive! Choose your own adventure; I'm just giving you a push in the right direction.

Universities

Universities are filled with highly trained, dedicated and intelligent people with the luxury of having time to think. Time is a necessary prerequisite when it comes to forecasting. Most universities are also happy to share their wisdom.

- **Cambridge University** (www.cam.ac.uk) puts out a weekly email summary of its research.
- **Harvard Business Review**'s long list of podcasts can be found at www.hbr.org/podcasts.
- **The Australian National University** has a similarly full list of podcasts, available at www.anu.edu.au/events/all-podcasts.
- *Research at Penn* is an annual publication of the **University of Pennsylvania**. Get it at www.upenn.edu/researchdir.

Consultants

Consultants are paid to be cleverer than their clients. Many of them display their cleverest ideas to attract business. You can benefit from their efforts.

- **McKinsey** (www.mckinsey.com), global management consultants, publishes interesting reports on just about everything.
- **Ipsos** (www.ipsos.com/en-au) and **SurveyMonkey** (rebranding to Momentive; www.surveymonkey.com) are two of the global

leaders in surveying and polling. Like McKinsey, they publish regular reports and blogs on all manner of interesting topics.

- **Good Judgement** (www.goodjudgement.com) brands itself as superforecasters. Check out its public dashboards (currently found under *Resources*).
- **Farnam Street** (www.fs.blog) is a wide-ranging and thought-provoking blog.
- **Futurist** is an international future-scanning consultancy. Sign up to its blog here: www.futurist.com/blog/.

Insurance

Insurers specialise in placing hefty bets on future calamities. If anyone knows what they're talking about, it's them. Pay attention to what they say, though take their considerations of human value with a grain of salt. After all, bankers aren't known for their esprit de corps.

- Global re-insurer **Swiss Re** publishes a wide range of reports through its Institute (www.swissre.com/institute/research.html).
- Global insurance giant **AXA**, in partnership with global researcher **Ipsos**, publishes an annual *Future Risks Report*, available here (www.axa.com/en/magazine/2020-future-risks-report).

Think Tanks

Similar to universities, think tanks are full of awfully smart cookies with time to contemplate matters.

- **Bruegel** (EU) – European economics think tank – "Bruegel's mission is to improve the quality of economic policy with open and fact-based research, analysis and debate". It has a range of podcasts, videos and data sets.

- **The Centre for Strategic and International Studies** (US) has a long list of podcasts, including *Unpacking Impact*, which "explores how rapid digital transformation shapes economics, culture, jobs, and public policy".
- **The Brookings Institution** (US) – "research topics cover foreign policy, economics, development, governance and metropolitan policy."
- **The Lowy Institute** (AU) – "an Australian think tank with a global outlook" – is Australia's most influential think tank, publishing podcasts and an insightful catalogue of polling data.
- **TED**, maker of the world-famous *TED Talks*, is not strictly a think tank but I'm including it anyway because of the quality of its content. As well as its enormous collection of TED Talks, it also has many fascinating and thought-provoking podcasts, one of which I'll reference in the next chapter. Check the collection out here: www.ted.com/podcasts.

DIY research

- Search "<your jurisdiction> projections" and see what your own government has to say. Also search for the levels above, below and beside you – local, state, regional, national, supranational.
- Search "<your jurisdiction> 2030" (or any other year) and see what comes up.
- Follow the industry bodies, community groups and other special interest groups that are relevant to your area. Industry bodies, in particular, usually publish periodic magazines, research or syntheses of their sector, including trends and risks. Gold mines!

Of course, this list isn't comprehensive, nor is it specific to your line of work. But it gives you the flavour of where to search out information.

So right now, put down this book and spend 10 minutes online working out some sources of future scanning that will fill in the right gaps for you.

2. LEARN TO RECOGNISE S-CURVES

Remember Uber from Chapter 17? When it launched in 2010, taxis had been around for centuries – first with legs, then engines.

And yet within five years, Uber had devastated taxis' share of the global ride-hailing market. Uber's disrupting technology had seemingly come out of nowhere to transform the industry.

But did it really come out of nowhere? In reality, Uber's rise followed a standard *S-curve*.

An S-curve describes the growth pattern of disruptions. The name refers to the shape that's created when you graph the uptake of a given thing over time. At first, there's very little uptake, then it gains momentum, til wham! Near-vertical growth. After a steep climb, the new thing has reached pretty much everywhere it's going to reach, and so the curve flattens off again.

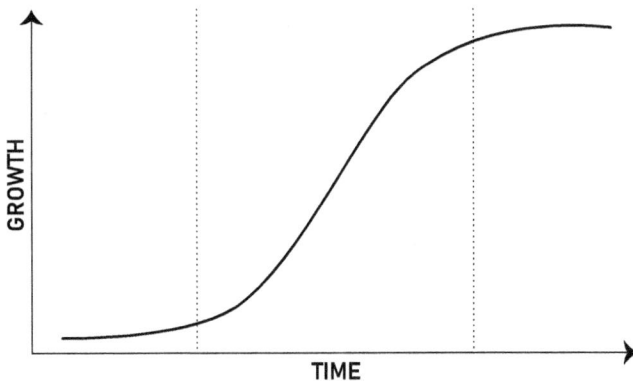

Figure 21.1: Standard S-curve

You're most likely to see S-curves being used to discuss new technology. iPhones followed an S-curve trajectory when they launched in 2007. Microsoft created an earlier S-curve when it first launched MS-DOS and then Windows in the 1980s. And electric vehicles are busily establishing an S-curve as I write this book.

Other things follow S-curves too. Sales of a band's latest album. Growth of algae in a pond. The total number of hugs you'll ever give your parents. Starts slow, picks up speed, then flattens off. Over and over again.

Have a look at this curve of global COVID-19 cases. It's not an S... yet. Hopefully by the time you're reading this, the curve has flattened out. But from here in 2022, that curve is still climbing.

Cumulative confirmed COVID-19 cases per million people

Due to limited testing, the number of confirmed cases is lower than the true number of infections.

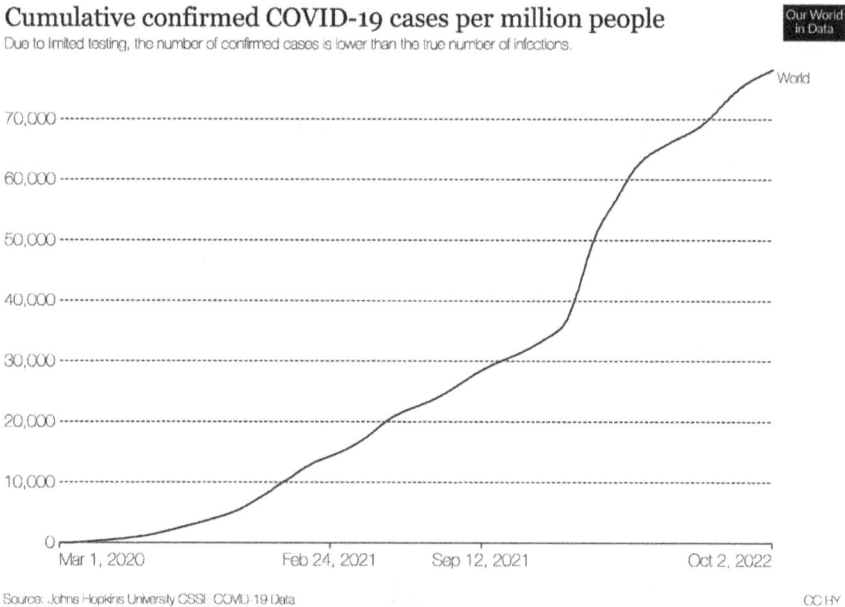

Source: Johns Hopkins University CSSE COVID-19 Data

OC HY

Figure 21.2: Cumulative confirmed COVID-19 cases

Here's another graph, this time charting the uptake of a whole range of "new" technologies in America throughout the 1900s and early 2000s. Lots and lots of S-curves, some with peaks and troughs along the way, and some so steep you could even call them "upside-down L-curves".

Share of US households using specific technologies, 1890 to 2019

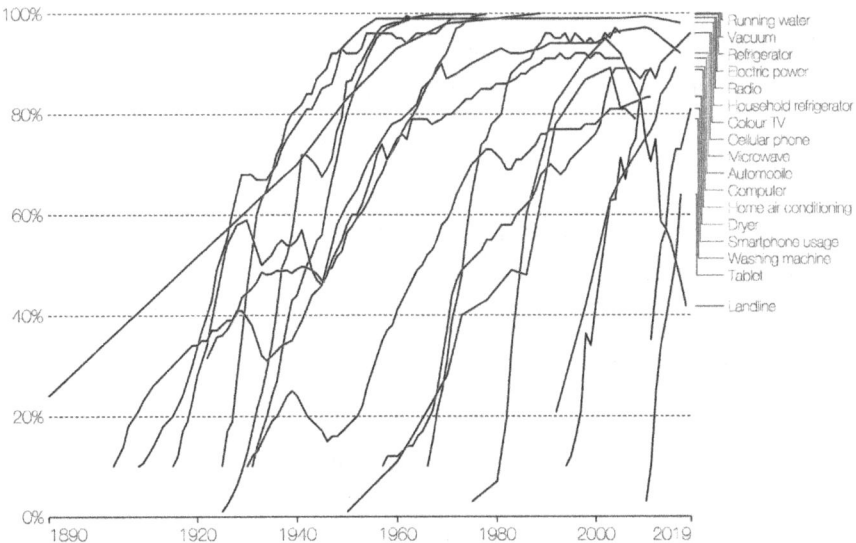

Figure 21.3: Adoption of technology in the US

Now it's worth pointing out that every single event, idea and thing can be charted into some sort of graph of its uptake over time. It's just that not all of them take on the S-curve shape. Some don't really have strong vertical climbs. Some climb for a while, but then instead of flattening off, they dive again. These aren't the curves that signal disruptions – disruptions come when the upward climb is steep and sustained. That's when you're seeing proper seismic change. That's an S-curve.

Early signs of S-curves include:

1. **Exponential growth:** track the rate the "thing" (product sales, infected patients, meteorite strikes) is doubling at. If that rate of doubling is steady or increasing, that's called exponential growth, and it takes numbers from tiny to huge, fast. Consider that if you start with only one thing, and that doubles every week, then in six months you've got over 30 million things.[1]

2. **Chatter:** if there's a lot of talk about the thing, whether that's among stakeholders, in the mainstream media or on social media, then it's a good sign that the thing could be reaching critical mass.

3. **Innovating on pain:** if the thing is bringing a totally new solution (innovation) to something that sucks (pain), and it's also generating either *exponential growth* or *chatter*, then it's likely to bend into an S-curve.

    While this might not appear to apply directly in, say, virology, that's because we look at it from our human perspective. The reason that an itty-bitty flu virus swept around the world in 2020 was because it was so new. While it caused pain to humans, if you look at it from the virus's perspective, the "innovation" at the heart of the virus – literally called the novel (new) coronavirus – was alleviating a major pain point for other flu viruses, because it had worked out a way around its hosts' immune system defences.

4. **Transmissability:** how readily the thing passes from one person to another. For a new idea, this will be a factor of how willingly people tell their friends and colleagues. For an illness, it's a biomechanical factor of how contagious the disease is.

Spotting S-curves isn't quite as easy as ticking off these criteria. As with so much in this book, your judgement remains crucial. But while these criteria aren't quite bulletproof, it's virtually impossible to get an S-curve without them. So learning to recognise the signs is a very useful part of your early warning system.

3. EXPLORE ALL ANGLES USING PESTLE

Throughout this part we've discussed the importance of understanding the context around you as you operate. But there's a lot to keep track of!

So here's a helpful acronym you can use to quickly brainstorm an issue from multiple angles: **PESTLE**. I didn't invent PESTLE, but I do use it often.

- **Political:** refers both to actual politicians, as well as media commentary, tension between key stakeholders and any other area where human disagreement may impact your thing
- **Economic:** refers to the financial costs and benefits of your thing, as well as the economic system in which it's operating
- **Social:** refers to the stakeholders, the community, human health and other people-based considerations (close relative to *political*)
- **Technological:** refers to the technical, data, engineering, mechanical details and constraints of your thing
- **Legal:** refers to the legal framework around your thing, including risks like liability or copyright
- **Environmental:** refers to the relationship between your thing and the land, air, water and living systems around it.

PESTLE is one tool with many uses. It's something you can use in a workshop setting to help spark exploration of a problem. It's also a tool you can run through in your head in a few seconds. I've even used it as the basis for a funding proposal.

For example, imagine you're working on a project to increase electric vehicle uptake in your city. You could use PESTLE to prompt yourself or your team to think about the barriers to uptake from various angles. Here's what that conversation might sound like…

- Political barriers:
    - Well, let's see, there's a problem with vehicle import tariffs. But from where we sit in local Council, can we change that? No. Moving on…
    - Next political problem. Our mayor doesn't like new things; he's a bit of an old fuddy-duddy. But we want to get a bigger budget to install a charging station. Can we do anything to get him onside? Yep, this is something within our control, let's add it to the list.
- Let's move on to think about economic barriers…

RECAP

- Foresight means you can be ready when change arrives. You can't prepare for what you can't see coming.

- Foresight isn't wizardry; it's a capability you can foster. Here are three practices that will help.

- First, borrow other people's brains. This means develop the habit of reading, watching and listening to what other (insightful) people have to say. Draw from a wide range of topics, even ones not obviously connected to your work.

- Learn to recognise S-curves as they're forming. S-curves describe the shape of change – slow at first, then a huge adoption of the change, then a plateau as the "new normal" arrives. S-curves are recognisable by exponential growth, chatter, innovating on pain and transmissibility.

- Brainstorm issues from multiple angles using PESTLE – political, economic, social, technological, legal and environmental. By reflecting on how an issue might have causes or consequences in each of these six big areas, you'll develop a greater understanding of the issues and won't be caught off guard.

YOUR TURN

1. Practise doing a PESTLE now, on a topic that's on your mind.

2. Listen to two new podcasts and subscribe to two blogs or newsletters.

22

How to turn disruptions into problems (you can solve)

A problem well put is half solved.

John Dewey, American philosopher

Remember at the start of this Part when I warned you about Superwoman/man Syndrome? This chapter will teach you the wisdom I had to have knocked into me the hard way. Do both of us a favour and learn from my mistake, okay?

Here's how I learned that biting off more than you can chew is dumb, and that learning how to scale problems to a solvable size is what the real pros do.

By early 2020 I'd been on hard burn for years. In fact, I'd been building up speed, piling more and more onto my plate – management roles, house renovations, elder care, a baby. Heck, I interviewed for an executive role from hospital, two days after giving birth! I got the job, but in hindsight, I was setting myself up for a fall.

From the outside I may have indeed looked like Superwoman, but inside, I was exhausted. The last straw came when my city was blanketed in smoke for weeks as the Black Summer fires tore across our country. Facebook showed me loved ones cowering in the waves under orange skies, clutching their terrified children. Friends and family in volunteer fire brigades across the country told harrowing stories of narrow escape. And on my doorstep, my own beautiful bush community braced to join the fight for our lives. By the time I limped into my last day of work in February 2020, I was emotionally exhausted.

My solution? I stopped. Like an alcoholic going cold turkey, I pulled away from all the responsibility that I could. My baby still got fed. Oh, and so did my sourdough starter – by this time it was COVID; there was no toilet paper but there was baking.

Thankfully, in April 2020 I had one of those wonderful turning-point conversations. My coach simply said, "Georgie, stop trying to fix the whole world by yourself."

I'm rarely speechless. But in that moment, I realised she was right. I'd been taking on every problem I encountered. And because of how my brain works, instead of reducing each problem down to a manageable size I'd been doing the opposite – seeing how everything connected to everything else, and seeking the one central thread that I could tug to unravel the whole mess. Because I believed that it was my responsibility to solve every problem around me, I was going insane trying, and failing, to get traction on all of it.

I drove bosses, colleagues and myself, nuts. I wish I had a dollar for every time someone told me to slow down. I'm exhausted now just thinking back to what it was like to be me back then!

So, I'm going to finish off this Part by teaching you how to translate a disruption into a **problem you can manage**. You can't start out your career going after climate change or global poverty – too big! **Walk before you run.**

It's time now for you to learn how to scale the systemic issues we've spoken about so far down to a size that allows you to squash a part of them (rather than them squashing you).

SCOPING PROBLEMS

I'm going to teach you the subtle, powerful art of *problem scoping*.

Problem scoping is about finding the right scale for your capability. It may seem like a pretty obvious step, but when you try it, you'll find that it's harder than you might think – unless you have a roadmap. **How you define a problem will change how you deliver the solution.**

As with many topics in this book, entire volumes have been written on scoping problems. But you and I both know that you don't have time to go read them all – you're already buried under a mountain of work!

So here is my synthesis of the best of the world's problem-identification thinking, mixed with my own years of experience, boiled down as ever to as pointed and useful a description as I can offer you.

In this chapter I'll teach you to identify problems with this catchy little pattern: **feel it, see it, weigh it, say it:**

- **Feel it** – connect to the harm caused by the problem
- **See it** – trace the harm back to its cause (or causes)
- **Weigh it** – recognise worthwhile opportunities for change
- **Say it** – put the problem succinctly into words.

But before I show you how to feel it, see it, weigh it and say it, I need to take a little side-quest to show you something really cool.

This next bit is one of my personal favourite distinctions anywhere in this book, or indeed in my career. I've been known to talk to strangers at dinner parties about this point. And the best part is they've loved it.

COMPLICATED VERSUS COMPLEX

The distinction between a *complicated problem* and a *complex problem* is one I use at least weekly, and have done so since the day I learned it. Credit goes to the *Cynefin Framework* (Cuh-neh-vin – it's Welsh) for drawing this critical distinction.

Here's the guts of the Cynefin Framework, in a tiny little nutshell. It lays out five types of problems – simple, complicated, complex, chaotic and disordered. These problems increase in difficulty, but there's more to it than that; they're also different in nature. I'll focus on explaining the part of the framework that will be the most useful to you now.[1]

Simple problems are, well, simple. They're the kind of problems with fairly obvious or easily discoverable solutions. For instance, "Does this citizen's driver's licence application meet the required criteria?" or "What's the best way to array the Bunsen burners to give the students the most space to work safely?"

The next two types of problems – complicated and complex – are the ones that you're going to encounter more and more as you move up the hierarchy. It's vital to recognise which is which, so you use the right tools.

Complicated problems

Complicated problems are those that, like simple problems, still have right and wrong answers, but the answers aren't immediately obvious.

Complicated problems abound in technical disciplines such as engineering, finance and medicine. For instance, "What's the minimum construction of a landfill lining to meet environmental requirements in this sensitive ecological area?" or "What caused the *Challenger* shuttle to disintegrate shortly after take-off?"

The answers may be hard to find, but they can be derived through diligent application of specialist knowledge. And importantly, the formula or process to answer the question in Scenario A applies to Scenario B, even if the variables are different. For instance, the investigators who worked out what went wrong with *Challenger* followed a very similar process to those who investigated *Columbia*.

Complex problems

Complex problems, by contrast, don't have clear-cut answers, and what works in one instance won't necessarily work in another. They're what I think of as "human problems" – messy, inconsistent, unpredictable and prone to change without notice.

Examples of complex problems include trying to get kids to avoid smoking – what works in Canada might not work in Australia, or what works in a private school may not work in a remote Aboriginal community because the social context, peer pressures and other influencing factors are completely different. So even though the health hazard of smoking is the same whether you're urban or rural, Aussie or Canadian, the public health campaign approaches may need to vary widely.

UNDERSTANDING THE DIFFERENCE

Now, why does it matter? There's an old saying that fits here:

> If your only tool is a hammer, everything looks like a nail,
> even if it's a grenade.[2]
>
> **Abraham Maslow**

It means, **we tend to view problems through the lens of what we know how to cope with**.

This is why there's an old engineering trope about how their solution to every problem is "more concrete". Or the joke I kicked off Chapter 6 with about economists – "assume a can opener".

Whether you're an engineer, an economist, a teacher, a systems administrator or any of the thousands of other professions in the public sector, the reality is that you'll deal with both complicated and complex problems. In fact, **many problems are actually both at once**.

If you only have the ability to recognise one, you're going to be in a world of hurt. Using the tools of one discipline – the metaphorical hammer – on the problem of another discipline – the grenade – well, it makes things go boom.

Let me give you an example from my own back catalogue.

Once upon a time, I managed two staff, whom I'll call Martin and Angela. Martin was a master of the complex – he could people like you wouldn't believe! I once asked him for a briefing on a contentious group of stakeholders, and the chat that I assumed would take two minutes went for half an hour. He meticulously explained every little foible, frustration, pressure point and sacred cow of each attendee. I've never been so well briefed on a group of people before or since.

No surprise that I assigned Martin to a very contentious, multi-stakeholder (aka complex) mess of a project. But the project had a large technical element (aka complicated), and he was really intimidated by that. He kept asking me to put someone else on the project, because he felt technically inadequate compared to the boffins in the room.

I kept telling him that the thing I needed him to solve was the relationship side – "go get them to agree a way forward!" But nothing I did could quiet his feeling that without a PhD in chemistry, he wasn't up to the task. Martin could *sense* the complicated elements of the project but couldn't *comprehend* them.

Contrast that with Angela. She was incredibly bright, a scientist of many years' experience. I assigned her to a problem of similar contentiousness and therefore complexity as Martin's, and with a similar level of technical complicatedness, too.

Well, her technical brain lapped up the complication, and yet, the project kept going off the rails. I'd get these howling phone calls from other stakeholders, but whenever I asked Angela how it was going, she'd always give me glowing reports.

Eventually matters got so bad I had to intervene, and I was finally able to work out the problem – Angela couldn't *see* the complexities, and thus was doing nothing to manage them! Unlike Martin, who could see the complication but was terrified of it, Angela had no idea that complexity was tearing her project apart.

Thus every time a worried stakeholder would approach her with a concern, she would patiently deliver a detailed technical explanation of what was being done to address the problem (as she saw it). That would leave her feeling she'd diligently done her job, while leaving the stakeholder's issues unresolved.

I'd like to say that with my new insight illuminating the path, I paired Martin and Angela together on both projects, and with their powers combined they nailed both. That would be a nice story, wouldn't it?

Unfortunately, Angela's project had gotten out-of-control enough that more drastic redistribution of resources was required, and not long after, Angela left my unit in high dudgeon. I never did succeed in helping her see complexity, though happily I had better luck teaching Martin how to cope with complication.

Now, the reality for most of us is that human problems – complex, messy, pains in the bum – are increasingly common, especially as we move up the hierarchy through our careers. It's why we spent a whole part of this book talking about stakeholders instead of statistics. And in fact, if you flip to any page in this book, you'll see far more discussion of complex matters (and how to navigate them) than of complicated ones.

That's because complicated problems, while important, are the kind of things that you can often look up in a textbook, technical manual or even just jump online – have you ever been talking to your GP and noticed them quickly searching how to treat your ailment online? That's because whether it's you with a splitting headache or me, the technical process to diagnose the cause is the same.

But even this example of a complicated problem – a splitting head-ache – can also have complexity sneakily hiding within it. To you the ailment might mean you'll have a hard time sitting an exam tomorrow, but for me, I'm scared witless because it looks like the start of the same illness that killed my mum (my mum is fine, by the way. This is just a hypothetical). So for our shared GP, that means that the same complicated issue can be accompanied by varying levels of complex-ity as the human element changes patient to patient.

So what's the lesson? Unless you're deep in the pure-research "ivory tower" of your organisation, **the nature of most modern problems is that they have *both* complicated and complex elements**.

That means if you're the type of person whose knowledge or preferences incline you toward complicated problems, you need to be mindful that the complex bits shouldn't be disregarded as irrelevant. As Angela found out, they can derail your endeavours, no matter how technically correct your work is.

And if you're the type to lean more toward complexity, you should recognise that the complicated bits will probably intimidate the hell out of you. Recognise that subject matter expertise is valuable, but so is the ability to build consensus, smooth ruffled feathers and resolve roadblocks. To this day I don't think Martin realised how huge an achievement it was when he got his rowdy group of stakeholders to actually *agree* to a way forward!

In short, whichever side of the fence your talents lie, know the other side is there, respect it, practise identifying which side your problem has landed you on in any given moment, and seek out people for your coalition that are happy dealing with the side you're weak on.

Now, let's get back to the main quest, with *feel it*.

1. HARM (Feel it)

One of the easiest ways to scope a problem is to look for harm. It's often easiest to start with harms because they're the thing we notice first.

Let's go back to that headache I was just talking about. Harms are the headache – the thing that grabbed our attention and made us decide to do something about it. **By exploring the harms in more detail, the underlying problems can become easier to spot.**

Some harm is obvious – muggings, failing students, fish stock depletion. Some harm is subtle or even hidden – for instance, it took decades for the link between smoking and lung cancer to be established.

The good news is that there are ways to make harms more obvious, once you know how to look.

Types of harm

Actual, potential and perceived. You've possibly heard these terms because they're used to describe bias, a common topic within government.

Some harm is **actual** – if you've been hit by a car on a pedestrian crossing, you've been harmed.

Some harm is **potential** – if the intersection is poorly lit and the pedestrian crossing is just after a tight corner, the potential for harm is pretty high.

Some harm is **perceived** – if the local residents who use the poorly designed crossing feel like they're in danger, then whether they get hit by a car or not, they're still stressing out and that's a harm in itself.

Look for the lumps

Harm can be found in data; in fact, as we move into the world of "big data", more and more insight can be gleaned from intelligent consideration of datasets. That's a book in itself, so for now I'll limit this vast topic to one point.

"Look for the lumps!" was a phrase I heard often from my wonderful boss back when I was running strategic compliance campaigns across Victoria at EPA. The "lumps" he referred to were clumps of problems from within a larger mess. In my case, instead of trying to stop all illegal waste dumping, we worked out where the lumps were – where the harm was highest – and poked there.

The same logic applies anywhere. Instead of trying to shorten average talk time on customer service calls by making every call shorter, how about exploring what makes the longest 10% so long and tackling that?

Here's a great example I encountered while I was cruising LinkedIn recently:

> Waste Reduction campaign – a recent report has found apples, bread, cheese, milk, meat and tomatoes are the major culprits in food waste, therefore reducing these foods will make a significant contribution.

That's a waste reduction campaign focusing on only six staple foods. Out of the whole household waste stream, why are they focusing on just six foods? Because those are the lumps.

Maybe you're wondering, aren't public servants supposed to make *everything* better? Well, no. The role of government, as we covered in Part 1, is to focus public resources on issues that affect the common good, and which can't be solved by other means. That still leaves you with plenty to choose from! And nobody has an infinite budget or infinite time – prioritisation is necessary.

By choosing problems from the lumps, you do a few things. First, by focusing on a high-harm problem, you get some impact! The Holy Grail! Your batteries will be refreshed, you'll earn some precious social license, and more people will want to work with you. Winning all round.

Second, you'll likely have reduced the overall harm by more than if you'd have put that same energy into trying to achieve a wider impact.

Doing a proper fix on one problem is better than a crap fix on five problems.

Third, you'll possibly have come up with a solution that you can replicate on other harms, especially if they're complicated (as opposed to complex).

Invisible harm

The final harm identification method I'll share is the opposite of looking for the lumps. It's to consider what's *not* in your data.

My favourite example of this is a story retold by Jordan Ellenberg in his excellent book, *How Not To Be Wrong*. The tale is of a WWII mathematician called Abraham Wald.

The story goes like this. Wald fled Europe and found haven throughout the war in the US government's Statistical Research Group. Ellenberg likens them to the statistics equivalent of the *Manhattan Project* (the top-secret group of physicists who developed the atomic bomb).

Here Wald was asked a fairly straightforward question by the US military – where should we add more armour to our planes?

See, planes would get riddled with bullet holes during combat, and so more armour meant more survivability. But it also meant more fuel consumption and less manoeuvrability. So there was a sweet spot; Wald's job was to find it.

Others had analysed the damage reports from returned planes, and had identified the areas most often hit. These were recommended for reinforcement. But Wald saw things differently.

His advice was to reinforce the areas *least* often hit.

Why? Because he saw what others didn't see – the missing planes.

The data the team was looking at was drawn from *the planes that returned*. Wald noticed that some areas of the planes were oddly under-represented in the damage data. Areas like the wings and the fuel tanks. He wondered why the returning planes weren't being shot there. The answer, he surmised, was that planes that got shot in such places didn't return.

So, reinforcement was placed in the critical areas that Wald identified, and pretty soon, planes started limping back to base with damage to the wings and fuel tanks – damage that had become survivable (just) thanks to the extra armour.

Wald saw the invisible harm, and he saved lives.

When examining problems, remember to ask – what's invisible? It's tricky to see the unseen though, so here are a few questions that can help:

- Whose voice isn't present in this discussion?
- Does the data represent the full spectrum of user/victim/client/ etc experience? (This is the kind of question we can assume Wald asked himself – "does the data I'm analysing take account of all planes that saw combat?" His answer was "no.")
- What would this situation look like if we were to place ourselves in the perpetrator/aggressor/other side's shoes?
- What couldn't happen because of what did happen/is happening?
- Whose voice is so loud it's drowning out the choir, and what does the problem sound like when we take that voice out of the mix (temporarily)?

2. CAUSE (See it)

You've heard the saying, "Treat the cause, not the symptoms". I just showed you how to get better at spotting the symptoms, so now let's consider how to trace those symptoms into their causes. An easy, intuitive method to do this is called a *root cause analysis*, but that's a painfully fancy term. I prefer to call it **Five Whys**. Why?

Because to get to the root cause of a problem, it's often as easy as asking "Why" a bunch of times. You'll feel like a three-year-old for a while, but there's a reason little kids ask questions – they're trying to understand how the world works.

Five Whys is easy – just keep asking why until you get to something where you see the all-important **opportunity for change** – a fairly self-explanatory term I'll nonetheless explain later.

Here's an example of how you might use Five Whys.

Lump: data from the last 12 months shows that there's been an uptick in the number of minor accidents at a local intersection. Hmm...

> *Why 1:* Why are there more accidents?
>
> *Answer 1:* A new school recently opened, so there's more distracted parents driving around there than before.
>
> *Why 2:* Why are the parents distracted?
>
> *Answer 2:* Because they're driving around in circles trying to find somewhere to stop.
>
> *Why 3:* Why do the parents need to stop?
>
> *Answer 3:* To drop off and pick up their kids.
>
> *Why 4:* Why is it so hard for them to stop?
>
> *Answer 4:* Because we foresaw the uptick in parents, so we put up lots of "no parking" signs so they wouldn't clog up the streets.

The Five Whys work because it's intuitive. It's also not limited to five; I used four in this example. Five is a good number because it can push you beyond the obvious.

You may go to seven Whys, then realise all of a sudden that you're talking about redesigning car collision avoidance systems, and maybe you've gone a bit too far. That's fine! Exploration is great.

Or maybe you get to three Whys, then find your answer – awesome! Part of the art of Five Whys is working out where the sweet spot is, and it's fine for that to be "three Whys ago".

3. OPPORTUNITY FOR CHANGE (Weigh it)

Now that you've identified some harm and worked out its cause, it's important to consider how to put boundaries around the problem so that you've got a realistic chance of fixing it.

This step is where you recognise that **within each big problem, there are smaller problems**. Some of the smaller problems are within your scope, and some aren't. Choose the ones that are.

Failure to do this step leads to getting squashed by hopeless quests.

If you're back to thinking about the increase in minor collisions at that local intersection, there's no use scoping your problem to be about poor car design if you're in the road maintenance division of your local Council. But you could scope a problem that's about poor road design, couldn't you?

Ranking opportunities

Some problems cause loads of harm and have clear causes, yet still have little opportunity for change without a lot of support. For instance, fossil fuel pollution – we know it kills, we know where the emissions come from, but good luck doing much about it unless you're in the right place.

But other problems are referred to as *low-hanging fruit* – problems that are easy to reach, easy to pick and full of juice.

A simple way to compare options is by creating a **Value for Effort Matrix**. Rank each option in terms of its relative value compared to the other options, and then its relative effort.

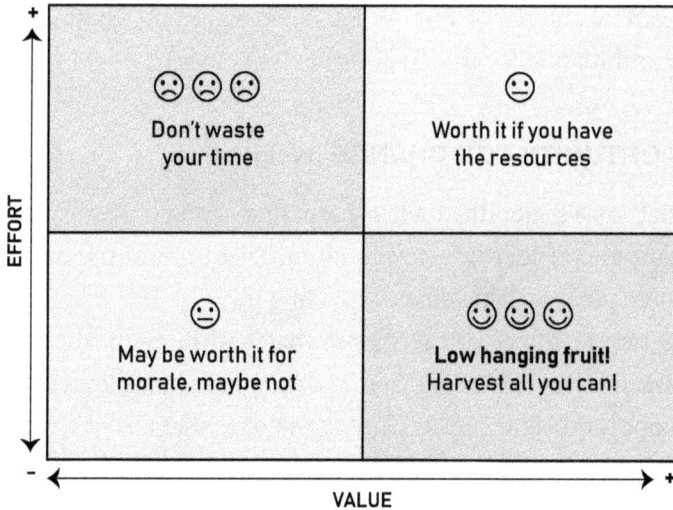

Figure 22.1: Value for Effort matrix

Remember, solving the pants off of a small problem is often more satisfying than making a tiny dent in a big problem.

Want proof? Go talk to anyone on the street and ask them what frustrates them right now. Odds are they'll tell you about their nagging spouse, their dripping kitchen tap, their aching feet, their annoying boss or any one of a number of personal, proximate issues.

Even when pollsters ask large populations what will shape their vote for the mob that'll lead our country for the next few years, the answers tend more to the personal than the global. The economy (my job) will almost always rank higher than wars, climate change or poverty – UNLESS those issues affect the surveyed people directly.

Fixing problems on a small scale will make a world of difference to the people whose problem you just fixed.

And every piece of experience you get adds to your tool kit. Your ability to deliver the Formula for Impact will be strengthened more by you practising on right-size problems than too-big ones.

4. STATE THE PROBLEM (SAY IT)

Now we arrive at the final piece of the puzzle for this Part, the moment when your "solvable problem, worth solving" emerges from the fog and stares you in the eye. The quote that started this chapter explains why **stating your problem** is a skill worth learning:

A problem well put is half solved.

Putting a clear box around your problem not only stops it growing so big that it squashes you, it also focuses the minds of the whole team around exactly what it is you're doing (and not doing).

If you read any book on problem solving, there will be discussion of a *problem statement.* They range in complexity. Of course, I want to give you a simple format you can pop in your mind-pocket to have ready wherever you go. This format captures what we've discussed in this chapter.

It's called the Six Ws: Who, What, When, Where, Why and Which (bit's ours).

First, state the Harm, using these specifics:

- **Who** is affected?
- **What** does the harm look like? What's the evidence?
- **When** did the problem start?
- **Where** is the problem likely to head, if left unchecked?

Then, explore the cause:

- **Why** do we think the problem is happening?

Then explore opportunities for change:

- **Which bit's ours:** our scope and resources allow us to consider this piece of the problem…

Here's an illustrative problem statement I wrote early in my career, when I was in a call centre process improvement role:

- *"Data analysis of incoming calls shows that older users age 65+* **(who)** *are 31% more likely to need to be redirected to the appropriate section for their inquiry, compared to younger users* **(what)**.

- *"Routine surveying shows that call misdirection is associated with a 25% decrease in user issue resolution and a 30% call dropout rate* **(what)**.

- *"Data for the last three years has shown this trend is increasing* **(what, when)**.

- *"Initial research indicates that older users get misdirected because they dislike interacting with IVRs ("press 1 to speak to…") so press random numbers til they get an operator* **(why)**.

- *"Given our aging user base, if left unaddressed, user dissatisfaction is likely to rise further* **(where)**.

- *"Increasing the IVR-literacy of our older users is beyond our scope. Therefore we recommend scoping our problem to be that the existing IVR content and layout is unsuitable for our older users* **(which bit's ours)**."

Here's a problem statement that needs work:

> "Older users have trouble getting to the right team member. They are frustrated and make complaints to management, which is lowering staff morale."

Aside from the sheer volume of the first example compared to the second, do you see how the first is also more specific and more evidence based? What other differences do you notice?

A great problem statement does so much of your work for you. Not only does it half-solve the problem by making the problem blindingly obvious, it also attracts powerful support because the arguments for change are baked in.

I love great problem statements!

RECAP

- It's all too easy to develop Superwo/man Syndrome when trying to close gaps.

- Learning how to choose the right-size problem for your capability and capacity is therefore a vital defence against getting squashed by too-big problems.

- The Cynefin Framework makes a useful distinction between complicated and complex problems.

- Complicated problems are technically challenging but solvable and replicable.

- Complex problems involve more interconnection, and changes in one part of the system have unpredictable consequences. Solutions to one complex problem usually only offer hints on how to solve similar problems.

- The nature of most public policy problems is that they include elements of both complication and complexity.

- Recognising each type of problem leads to better problem solving.

- People who prefer complex problems tend to be intimidated by the technical nature of complicated problems, and thus can become stuck or overwhelmed.

- People who prefer complicated problems tend not to recognise complex problems, and thus tend not to manage them effectively.

- To scope "solvable problems worth solving", use the "feel it, see it, weigh it, say it" method.

- Detect problems (feel it) by recognising actual, potential and perceived harms. Remember to look for both the lumps and the invisible harms.

- Identify the cause of problems (see it) by asking Five Whys to get to the root cause.

- Carve out manageable pieces of problems (weigh it) by considering the opportunity for change. Use the Value For Effort Matrix to clearly compare options.

- Articulate a clear problem statement (say it) using the Six Ws Method. Remember that a clear problem statement offers clarity and will help you attract the right support to deliver.

YOUR TURN

Choose a project and write a problem statement for it. This can be a project you're working on now, one you've done in the past or one you want to do.

1. **Feel it:** what's the harm? Actual, potential and perceived? Are there lumps? Invisibles? Can you use a HEAT Sheet or HEAT Map here to give you some more angles on your stakeholders' perception of harms?

2. **See it:** bust out those Five Whys. Do them in your head, or better yet, talk to people! If this is a real problem you're working on now, this is a great chance to build up some stakeholder love and add to your coalition.

3. **Weigh it:** do a Value For Effort Matrix to see where the real opportunities are for change.

4. **Say it:** bring your work together into a tight problem statement. Make it sing! You want a problem statement to land on the desk of a decision-maker with a resounding thud – once they read it, they can't help but back you.

WRAPPING UP PART 4

This Part has been big. We've explored the drivers of disruption, and what the public expect you to do about it. We've checked out some of the biggest global disruptions, then examined how to connect those macro issues to your daily work. We've given you a lot of tools, too – tools to seek, identify and understand disruptions, then carve out manageable problems.

Taking a planet-sized view can be overwhelming. Maybe you feel like you're just one little person; what difference can you make?

But remember, don't try to solve climate change or drug cartels or election fraud today. Those are really, *really* big problems. Building up to those by cutting your teeth on smaller, simpler, more readily solvable problems will not only enable you to go further, faster. It'll also make a huge difference to people in your community, here and now. I promise.

THAT'S NOT ME

Before we go onto Part 5, I want to talk to you for a minute about a concern you might be having. Even at this point, you still might not see yourself as a change-maker. Perhaps you're not into that, or perhaps you don't think your role involves delivering change. I'm going to challenge both those ways of thinking.

The term "change" has been used a lot in recent years to refer to grand things – be the change you want to see in the world, climate change and so on.

But strip it back, and change simply refers to something going from state-of-being A to state-of-being B.

Even maintenance is change. To maintain a road in good working order, you'll occasionally need to resurface it – that's a change. To maintain your organisation's website, you'll need to periodically review and update it – another change.

Doing process roles such as assessing applications involves change – the application goes from pending to under assessment to finalised. And the applicant goes from hopeful to impatient to happy (or frustrated, depending on the decision). Change, change, change.

But... changes are all different, right? Changing your office's tea supplier is hardly the same as changing your government's refugee policy.

Actually...

While every change has its own characteristics, the truth is – **delivering change is always the same.**

ALL change delivery projects, huge or tiny, follow the same pattern. I call that pattern the *Delta,* and it forms the backbone of **the fifth and final P – the right Process.**

PART 5

PROCESS

How to deliver change people respect

There is nothing permanent except change.

Heraclitus

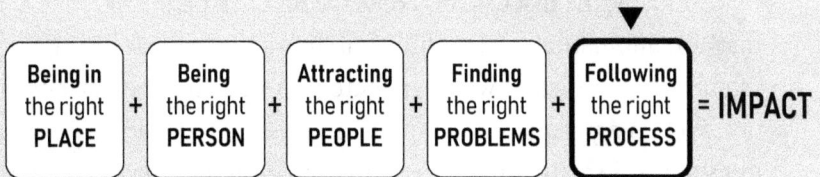

Back in 2010 as I joined the EPA, there was a lot of community unrest in the vicinity of a particularly nasty landfill here in Melbourne. Residents had noticed they were getting weird cancers. The culprit, according to general opinion, was the landfill.

It was EPA's job to police landfills. The community around that particular landfill felt their concerns had been ignored by EPA for a long time, and they weren't putting up with it any more. A reckoning was brewing, fast.

I was lucky to bear witness to what happened next.

Our brand-new CEO did something I'd never seen anyone do before (or since). He went out there, to community meetings, and he listened. I mean, *he really listened.* In fact, for months, he'd front up to these meetings, stand on stage, and get shouted at. For hours. Over and over.

Eventually, everyone had their vent. Then, our CEO was able to move on to the next phase of his plan. He invited the leaders of the various community groups to join him on a working party. Together, they started actually talking (not shouting).

My CEO asked the community leaders what they wanted, then listened to their answers. He probed, pushed, guided them to unpack the real concerns underpinning all the shouting. And make no mistake, those concerns were very real. If you think that there's a cancer source lurking in your suburb, wouldn't you be concerned, too?

Gradually, the discussions converged on to a plan. Everyone agreed that a combination of landfill sampling and medical testing would establish scientifically whether there was indeed a cancer cluster or not. So EPA agreed to do comprehensive land, water and air sampling to establish exactly what emissions were coming out of the landfill. EPA also got the Department of Health to agree to take bloods and do health surveys with residents.

Fast forward about a year. The EPA and Department of Health staff had done the agreed testing, and they'd sent all the results off to an independent third party to review and report.

The day comes that the report is handed back. After months of holding their breath, everyone was keen to know the truth.

The findings were clear – there was no cancer cluster. The landfill was operating well within safety margins, and while there were definitely members of the community with cancers of all sorts, that was also well within normal parameters for the population.

Here's the thing that I'll never forget. The community that had been so furious with EPA for years and years, who had shown up in droves to scream at the CEO, and who were so frightened and felt so abandoned – guess how they reacted?

They said, "Okay". They were grateful. *They thanked us.*

Not every last person. And not every "okay" was said with much enthusiasm. But the reality was that they accepted that the results were fair, and they were willing to let that be the end of the matter.

The leader of the campaign was a woman who had been thought for years to be totally unmanageable and who had joined the working party through gritted teeth. Well, she stood up at the community meeting where the results were announced, and said to her people, "I believe in this report, and as much as it's not what we expected, I support the findings." I'm paraphrasing, of course, but you get the drift.

The lesson to me was crystal clear. **When you deliver change the right way, people will respect the outcome, even if they don't always like it.**

Everything I've taught you so far has been about giving you the mindset, knowledge and skills you need to make things change from how they are now to how you want them to be.

Now that those foundations are in place, it's time to bring it all together to close the gaps that matter to your community.

In these final chapters we'll unpack the Delta change model. We'll explore a legal concept that encapsulates the Public Sector Principles. Then we'll use that legal concept to put a spin on the Delta that'll ensure you can always bring people along, building up social license and ensuring that the changes you deliver actually work.

By the end of this Part, you'll have everything you need to close gaps today and for years to come.

23

The blueprint for all change

To live is to choose. But to choose well, you must know
who you are and what you stand for, where you want to go
and why you want to get there.

Kofi Annan, UN Secretary-General and Nobel Peace Prize winner

Recently I ran a workshop on the other side of town. I jumped in my car, and did what 99% of us do when we head somewhere new – opened Maps on my phone to work out how to get there.

It occurred to me as I drove away that I'd just done a **Delta** – a change.

Now, you may be asking why I call this a Delta. Weird word choice, especially since COVID made it a dirty word.

Delta is a Greek letter (Δ or δ), and it's used in mathematics to denote... you guessed it... change.

For instance, a common mathematical notation is ΔT, which stands for "change over time".

To deliver any change, you must achieve three things:

1. Establish where you're at now
2. Decide how to get where you want to go
3. Get there.

Later that day I facilitated the workshop, helping the participants move through a complicated, complex problem to gain clarity on how to proceed. We started by agreeing on the current state of play for their problem. Then we held a wide-ranging discussion on what ideal futures everyone saw for the problem. Eventually we converged on a shared future vision, then set about working out exactly how to get there. The workshop ended with a long list of assigned actions, as workshops often do.

Driving home, I reflected that I'd guided the group to:

1. Establish a shared understanding of where they were at now
2. Decide where they wanted to go and how to get there
3. Agree who was doing what to actually get them there.

Look at those two numbered lists – they're basically the same thing. And both Deltas.

Of course, that workshop followed the Delta pattern not by chance but by design – this ain't my first rodeo.

It was still nice to remind myself how Deltas crop up time and time again – from facilitating project design workshops to navigating across town – the blueprint for change is the same.

CHANGE IS ALWAYS THE SAME

The Delta change model is my own adaptation of a formula that you'll see used in most change management training the world over: *discover, design, deliver.*

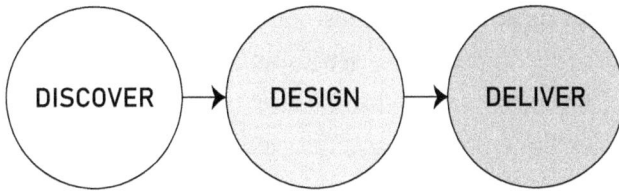

Figure 23.1: Discover, design, deliver model

This basic model applies equally to whether you're heading to a party or processing speeding fines or redesigning your country's postal voting scheme.

In fact, if you Google "discover, design, deliver", you'll find versions applied to everything from software design to IT sales, boatmaking to road construction.

Why does this same pattern crop up everywhere? **Because the pattern of making change is universal.**

So while there's value in zooming into individual industries, you and I both know that public servants are working to create stable environments for *every* industry. There are public servants doing just about every type of work imaginable for pretty much every industry in Australia.

So rather than teach you a change process for the resources industry, regional development or women in sport, I'll show you the universally applicable model! Then you can take it with you no matter where your career takes you.

YOUR INTERNAL GPS

Teaching you the universal architecture of change is valuable not just so that you can deliver change projects in lots of different roles. The real value is this – **by internalising this process, you can never get lost**.

What do I mean by getting lost? You can still get lost if you try to drive across the Simpson Desert without a GPS, so don't do that.

What I mean by never getting lost is this – the more complicated and complex your projects get, the easier it is to get into a state of confusion.

If you remember back to the Cynefin Framework that we discussed in Chapter 22, you may recall that I mentioned two more types of problems after *simple, complicated* and *complex*. Those were *chaotic* and *disordered*.

Well, chaotic and disordered problems generate lots of "what on earth is going on here?" moments. They're no fun. You may yet encounter those later in your career, because big problems are very often chaotic or disordered.

By having the Delta change model burned into your brain though, you're far more likely to be able to navigate through *all* types of problems in a calm, unruffled way. Why? Because no matter what the problem is, if you can simply stop and ask yourself (and others) to first decide what step you're at, and then to agree on whatever that step is asking you to do, then you're able to maintain a degree of control no matter what.

And as you'll learn throughout your career, staying calm when all around you is stormy will lead you to better decisions, smarter action and a helluva lot of recognition.

I STILL DON'T GET IT

We'll look more closely at these three basic components, so that you become familiar with the pattern. Let's go back to me mapping myself to that meeting.

As soon as I opened Maps, it pinged my location. Bam, that's *discover*.

Next, I punched in the address of the meeting, and was presented with route options to choose from. That's *design*.

Finally, I set off, and Maps tracked me as I went. I got turn by turn directions, and when I went off course, I got rerouted. That's *deliver*!

Now what if I had location services turned off? That would've made it impossible to find a route.

And if instead of an address I just entered a suburb, then the route I got shown would've gotten me close but not quite there.

This illustrates a critical point – **every step of the Delta, in order, is vital to successful change**.

At this point, you're probably thinking, "You're trying to tell me that I can solve huge problems just by identifying three things?"

Well yes, and no. Those huge messes need more sophistication than three simple questions, but that's the beauty of Deltas – we can build on that basic three-step architecture to deliver anything.

In the same way, there are only 26 letters in the English alphabet but hundreds of thousands of words. And houses only have a few types of rooms – kitchen, bathroom, bedroom, etc – but endless layouts.

No matter how complicated the change model, every single one will follow the exact same basic architecture of discover, design, deliver. Every time.

RECAP

- All change processes have the same basic architecture.
- By learning it, you will be able to make sense of messy situations.
- The basic architecture of all change is the Delta change model: discover, design, deliver.
- Discover means to establish where you're at now.
- Design means to decide how to get to where you want to go.
- Deliver means to get there.
- Each step must be performed in order, or else impact isn't guaranteed.

YOUR TURN

1. Think of a change, any change, then identify the three Delta steps within it.

   How about making your breakfast this morning?
   - I'm hungry.
   - I want to be full of toast.
   - Make and eat toast.

   Or asking for a day off?
   - I need a mental health day.
   - Decide which day is most likely to be approved.
   - Ask boss for the day off.

2. Identify five Deltas you've run today at work and explore their three steps.

24

The shortest route to failure is to forget fairness

Being good is easy, what is difficult is being just.

Victor Hugo

The joy of the Delta change model is that it can be infinitely customised.

When we think about how to tailor a Delta to design our **fifth P – a process to deliver change within the public service**, I can think of no better guide than the other four Ps.

Way back in Part 1 I laid out the Public Sector Principles. In Part 2 I made the distinction between success, power and impact. In Part 3, I introduced you to the profoundly important idea of social license. In Part 4 I laid out what people expect of their governments.

If I had to boil all of my wisdom on how to achieve impact down to one word, it would be this: **fairness**.

Let me make my point with a story.

A friend of mine, Kathy, once received three speeding tickets in three days. All three were for doing 58km/hour in a 50km/hour zone.

Kathy was flabbergasted; she was a conservative driver with an unblemished record, so these tickets copped some serious side-eye.

It turned out that Kathy's route to drop her kids at school had recently been rezoned from 60km/hour down to 50km/hour. Fair enough, except that there was no "new speed limit" signage. The speed signs themselves had changed but that was it.

So for locals like Kathy, there was very little chance they would notice the change. Do you meticulously read every sign on your daily commute?

Now Kathy wasn't short of a dollar, so she could've just paid up. But she felt they were unfair, so guess what she did? Yep, she disputed all three.

When her day in court arrived, Kathy pleaded her case. After hearing both sides, the judge decided that because there was nothing alerting drivers to the reduced speed limit, Kathy had no reasonable way of knowing she needed to change her behaviour, and so the police couldn't penalise her.

The judge threw all three fines out, on the grounds that Kathy wasn't given procedural fairness.

PROCEDURAL FAIRNESS

You might have heard of the "pub test". Which is to say, if you told your mate about something the government was doing over a beer down at the pub, would your mate reckon it was fair? What happened to Kathy failed the pub test.

Fairness (as in Kathy's case), described by the legal concept of procedural fairness (which is sometimes called natural justice), is something instinctive to all humans, even babies. In fact, studies have even shown that other primates such as chimpanzees have a well-developed sense of fairness, too.

The question for us now becomes how do we deliver a Delta dripping with fairness? In fact, so very fair that we can rightly call it **The Fairness Delta**? I'll spend our final three chapters teaching you how.

RECAP

- The Delta change model can be customised to suit its user's case.

- The overarching concept that unites everything we've discovered together in this book is fairness.

- Fairness, therefore, is the foundation of the fifth P – a process to deliver change within the public service.

- Humans and even other primates have an innate sense of fairness.

YOUR TURN

1. Think of a time when something happened to you that you think was unfair. Unpack that now, referring back to the concepts recapped in this chapter.

2. What concepts describe the unfairness best?

25

Discover

Always strive to be more interested than interesting.

Jane Fonda

Back when my son was just learning to talk, he woke up screaming one night. My dear husband went to see what was wrong. A minute later he re-entered our bedroom with little Hugo shrieking, "Bad dad! Bad dad!" and trying to escape. "Bad Dad" immediately handed Hugo to me for comfort. But even then, Hugo just kept shouting it over and over.

Abruptly, my husband leapt out of the room. I thought he'd finally had enough of being told off by our tiny tyrant, but moments later he materialised with Hugo's blanket.

"BAD DAD!" Hugo jubilantly exclaimed, grabbing his blanket tightly and instantly calming. Turns out the blanket had fallen out of his cot, which was why he was crying. "Bad dad" equalled blanket. Huh.

That night our son cried because we'd been trying to solve the wrong problem – we misunderstood our key stakeholder. As soon as my husband stopped hearing what *he thought* Hugo was saying, and started seeing the world from our tiny kid's perspective, understanding dawned and the solution became clear.

That's why the Delta change model starts with discovery. Until you know how things *really* are, you're in no position to do anything about it.

WHERE ARE WE?

When we're discussing mapping ourselves to a meeting or even calming a shrieky toddler, there's not a huge amount of debate.

But for the kind of problems that you're going to deal with as a public servant, "where are we?" can be a hotly contested topic. If you're asking about, say, the state of the federal highway system, every person you ask will have a different view.

For a simple question, "where are we?" sure can be hard to answer. I find it easier to break "where are we?" into two halves – "how is it now?" and "how'd we get here?".

HOW IS IT NOW?

To answer "how is it now?", hunt down the objective, clear-eyed statements that describe the situation you're examining.

Look for the **what's-so statements** – objective, uncontroversial. The what's-so statements act as a stable foundation from which to have a reasoned discussion with different stakeholders.

This includes both facts and opinions – a point which aligns quite neatly with the *complicated/complex* distinction of the *Cynefin Framework*. Facts are testable; opinions are human. Both matter greatly.

Facts will act as a stable foundation from which to have a reasoned discussion with different *stakeholders* when you get to the design step. For example, let's say you're exploring highway infrastructure preparedness; in that case, the statement "Australia's population is 25M people and growing" is a great fact to serve as a starting point.

Opinions, meanwhile, can shed light on areas that facts might not reveal. If, say, the head of the truckers' union says, "Our highways are heaps worse than they were 30 years ago", that may or may not be objectively true, but if he thinks it's true, that still matters.

Opinions are, of course, subjective but they can still beget facts. For instance, "there is a demonstrated gap between measurable highway infrastructure quality and key user groups' perceptions".

An area where facts and opinions merge is in *expectations*. The risks people think you should be *minimising* and the benefits you should be *maximising* will all be embedded within the facts and opinions you tease out.

HOW'D WE GET HERE?

Any consideration of how a situation is now must include consideration of where it came from and how it went from there to here. **There is no such thing as Day Zero – everything has a history.**

The more that you understand how things were, the more you understand *why* things are as they are now. Consider questions like "What were the infrastructure budget allocations in the last 30 federal budgets?" or "How politically contested was highway infrastructure spending in each of the last three elections?" Keep your eyes peeled for issues that might signal that an inner *ESE* sphere is encroaching on an outer sphere.

Another quirk of understanding how you got where you are is that you'll often encounter the ghosts of attempts past. The road to hell is paved with poorly executed old projects. Keep your ears open for previous attempts to appease noisy stakeholders – places where *want* was prioritised over *need*. Look for *externalities* that have been overlooked. Remember your job is to deliver what's *worthy*, not just what's *sexy* or *expedient*.

Once you understand *how* the past became the present, you're in a strong position to make predictions about *where* the situation is headed in the absence of any intervention. "We've established that heavy vehicle movements are steadily increasing. We're also observing that damage from climate change related weather events is increasing. Therefore, without a change to expenditure or maintenance methods, the rate of overall infrastructure deterioration is likely to accelerate."

Notice how that reads awfully like the beginnings of a *problem statement*?

HOW DO I FIND OUT?

By now I probably don't need to tell you that the way you establish the how'd-we-get-here of the situation is by listening to your stakeholders.

"You work in infrastructure integrity testing; how would you categorise our existing interstate highway infrastructure?" or "As a heavy vehicle driver, do you find the current state of our highways adequate?" Listening will gather both facts and opinions.

While you're listening, you can be on the lookout for *HEAT* scores, and checking for signs of *S-curves* brewing.

WHEN DOES DISCOVERY STOP?

Throughout the discover step, you should be trying to get agreement on as many points as you can. "Can we agree that the current level of highway infrastructure is unlikely to service a population of 35M people?" Do this by using your positional *power* and personal *Ikigai* insight to be a *synthesiser*.

Where you can't find agreement, try to at least agree on where there is disagreement. "There's disagreement from stakeholders on the extent to which autonomous trucks will reduce highway deterioration rates. Given the rapid development and uptake of autonomous trucking fleets internationally, this is a matter that warrants further exploration to establish relevance to the Australian context."

Discovery doesn't have to go on forever. Part of the art of being a great public servant is honing your judgement. That includes learning to recognise when the important people in a problem feel heard and thus, open to change.

Discovery is done when you can form up a clear *problem statement* that your stakeholders can largely agree with.

WHY BOTHER?

When you think about the kind of problems you deal with now, they may not feel like they warrant much effort in the discover step. Perhaps you think it's enough for you to resolve any "where are we?" questions for yourself.

However, no matter how simple the problem, discovery is also a chance to start building your coalition of support by letting them in at the beginning of a project.

So, don't hog the mike – let others have their say.

RECAP

- The kind of problems facing public servants tend to warrant putting effort into the discover step.

- Discovery is the perfect time to start forging coalitions of support.

- The discover step is all about reaching agreement on "where are we?"

- "Where are we?" breaks down to "how is it now?" and "how'd we get here?"

- Discovery ends when you've got an agreed problem statement.

YOUR TURN

1. Think about a problem you've dealt with recently. What discovery actions did you take? Do you think they were enough to meet your stakeholders' sense of fairness? If not, what signals have you received that give you that indication? What do you think you could feasibly have done differently?

2. If you think you met your stakeholders' sense of fairness, how do you know? What ways would exceed their expectations? What do you think it might take to get them to tell their mates at the pub about how impressed they were with your handling of the matter?

3. Remember that being *fair* isn't about doing what's *popular*. The landfill cancer report I told you about at the start of this Part didn't confirm the popular opinion. But it met and even surpassed everyone's expectations of fairness. What would that feel like for your work?

26

Design

Do what is right, not what is easy.

Anonymous

The discover step was all about establishing how things are – "where are we, and how did we get here?"

The design step is about deciding how we want things to be – "where are we going, and how do we get there?"

Sometimes the relationship between where we are and where we want to be is obvious; if you have a headache, you probably just want the pain to stop. But for more complex matters – including most public policy – every man and his dog will have a different view on how things should be.

So, how do you make sense of all that? More to the point, how on earth do you chart a course through those treacherous waters to deliver work that people respect, even when it doesn't deliver exactly what they wanted?

Good thing we're talking.

WHERE ARE WE GOING?

Here's the truth; good design is hard. If it were easy, we wouldn't have problems any more, would we? But this isn't *somebody else's problem*; it's yours.

Answering the question of "where are we going?" requires you to define *success* to reflect *impact*. **Get specific, and get agreement.** That lays a strong foundation for building *social license*.

Easier said than done. Here are three inconvenient yet important truths to remember as you go:

1. **Clear paths are uncommon.** The more important the subject, the wider the spectrum of opinion will be on what should happen. That's because all the stuff that's both important and widely agreed on is already baked into the fabric of our society. Ideas like "murder is unhelpful" or "children shouldn't work down mines". The problems you're left with, therefore, tend to be either small or contentious. Start with small; work up to contentious. And always expect it to be hard. Remember to apply your judgement to evaluate each *stakeholder's* view.

2. **Choices must be made.** After discovery, you'll have a lot of options on the table. Some stuff is easy to eliminate – too costly, too slow, too unpalatable. You may still have to choose between equally worthy options or equally terrible ones. Be guided by the *Public Sector Principles* and your *head of power*, so you have a solid defence for the tough calls. Remember that your citizens expect you to *foresee disruption* to *minimise cost* and *maximise benefit* by considering *value for effort*.

3. **Compromise is a virtue.** Compromise is the art of first balancing, and then selling, the wins and the losses. *Synthesise*

win-wins wherever possible. Make peace with the fact that sometimes no-one will love the choices you make.

PUBLIC SECTOR PURPOSE

To deliver what your jurisdiction needs to thrive.

PUBLIC SECTOR PRINCIPLES

1. Commitment to jurisdiction
2. Integrity and ethical conduct
3. Fairness and impartiality
4. Accountability
5. Human rights
6. Leadership
7. Effectiveness

HOW DO WE GET THERE?

Plan, plan, plan. Beyonce was wrong; girls don't run the world – plans do.

It's not enough to simply decide the right course of action. If you don't work out how to get there, then you'll get nowhere. Planning is your opportunity to work through what to do, how to do it, and why – before you're in the thick of it.

Plans separate the decisions about what needs to be done from the time pressures of getting it done. This prevents the enemy of the *common good – expedience* – from ruining your good intentions.

As they say, plan your work (design), then work your plan (deliver).

Your organisation almost certainly has a planning template. Use it. But don't mindlessly complete each section. **Plans are story-telling instruments.** So pour the results of all of your *synthesis* into your plans.

You can articulate the *disruptions* affecting your project by showing *Causation Maps*. You might use *PESTLE* to shape a risk assessment. Your *problem statement* is a place to show you've done the thinking on the *harms*, the *cause* and the *opportunity for change*.

WHEN DOES DESIGN STOP?

You're safe to move to action once your plan meets three tests:

1. **It's sensible:** you've satisfied yourself there's enough evidence to believe the plan will work.
2. **It's agreed:** your stakeholders support the plan.
3. **It's approved:** the necessary resource controllers have signed off on the plan.

WHY BOTHER?

Maybe you don't get to design solutions just yet – you're early in your career, so it's conceivable that you're simply being told what to do every minute. But by now I'm sure you remember that you already have some say over what you do, through your *discretionary effort*.

Here's the thing. Every single task you do is a Delta. Something needs doing, it gets assigned to you to do, and then you do it. Maybe 90 per cent of the design is already decided for you, but you still get to determine if it's done well or poorly, sloppily or neatly, quickly or slowly, pleasantly or unpleasantly. So you can practise now on low-risk tasks, and build up the skill for when it counts later on.

You probably won't do everything every time – I don't. The point is to have lots of tools in your kitbag that you know how to use well when the job calls for it.

RECAP

- The design step requires you to decide "where are we going, and how do we get there?"

- Public policy is a hotly contested space; opinions on how to close gaps abound.

- As a public servant, you'll continually be called upon to exercise judgement in making difficult choices fairly.

- The hard truth is that clear paths are uncommon, choices must be made, and compromise is a virtue you'll need to master.

- The way that decisions become actions is with clear plans.

- Plans are first and foremost storytelling instruments.

- You're ready to move into delivery once your plan is sensible, agreed and approved.

YOUR TURN

1. Go find your organisation's project management template. Spend time now getting familiar with it.

2. Where would you put your *problem statement*? *HEAT Sheet* and *HEAT Map* (or an analysis thereof)? How and where would you reference the *Public Sector Principles*?

3. Save the template to your personal drive if you have one. Jot yourself some notes using the Comments function, to remind you next time you need it.

27

Deliver

In theory, there is no difference between theory and practice.
In practice, there is.

Yogi Berra, 20th-century baseball player and coach

So, you've planned the work. Here in the deliver step, you work the plan. Because **designing without doing is just dreaming**.

Years ago, I worked on a road project that went through four design iterations across different governments before they ever turned the first sod. We mapped routes, did public consultation, made construction plans... only for the next government to chuck it in the bin and start again.

All four iterations had their merits and drawbacks – none were perfect. But of those four, the only one that ever made a single iota of difference, despite its shortcomings, was the one that got built.

Life is comfortable when we're planning – all the anticipation of fixing problems (and the announceables!), without any of the messy bits. But you've got to go out there and do the thing, otherwise those gaps will stay open.

ACTUALLY ACT

The deliver step is all about, well, action. It's where you follow the plan from your design step, to move toward your goal. As The Doors say, "the time to hesitate is through".

The bigger the project, the more time you'll have just spent in discovery and design. Both of those are "thinkie talkie" tasks, and can get very comfortable. But as I said above – if you don't actually do some stuff, then, well, nothing actually gets better.

Remember as you act to focus on *what your jurisdiction needs*. Your job is to create a *stable operating environment* within which your citizens can flourish. To both do good, and be seen to do good, so that your agency's *social license* increases, citizens know they're being taken care of, and you and your agency can achieve more and more good as a result. Whether you do this by *delivering services* or *regulating*, never be afraid to put your good work on *blast*.

It's easy to be scared of the action step. Even if you're not, your boss might be. Because do you know what action can get you? Criticism. So, read on for two ideas that reduce the risk of acting.

ITERATE WITH INTENTION

The best deliveries get redesigned as they go. Even simple problems don't always have obvious solutions. So while of course you give it your best guess in design, there is no substitute for the feedback you get when you try your ideas out in the real world.

The worst thing you can do as an aspiring gap-closer is to plough on with Plan A regardless of early delivery results. Yet I've seen this happen more often than I'd care to recall.

Never be afraid to change course as the facts change.

LEARNING MINDSET

Recognising opportunities to iterate requires you to be humble, curious and flexible. Without these characteristics, iteration is impossible. And without iteration, success is unlikely.

If you've taken Part 2 to heart, humility, curiosity and flexibility should come naturally to you. They will support your development of an *internal locus of control* and guard you against turning into *toxic waste*. Bonus.

WHY BOTHER?

Discover, design, deliver is a game changer, if you let it be. It's instinctive – just listen, plan, then do – three things that every human is capable of.

If you're feeling overwhelmed thinking about applying this level of thought to your work, please, don't be. Going through this process doesn't have to be *War and Peace*. With practice, this will become something that you can do automatically. I speak from experience.

Here's what it often sounds like in my head: "Hang on, this conversation is important. What are the what's-so statements? Is this corroborating what others have told me or contradicting it? What might be the way through this problem? What are the trade-offs? Who could I test that with?" You can do that in a few minutes, right?

By practising the process on the small stuff now, when you work your way up – which you will – you've got the experience you need to do these steps naturally. You will do it instinctively in the same way as you can run to the bus without tripping over your feet. You couldn't always run, but you practised, fell over a bunch, then got better and better. Well, same here. Practise now, on the proverbial carpet, so that by the time you're on the concrete and running, you'll trust your legs.

RECAP

- Designing without doing is just dreaming. So, do the thing.

- Take action, then observe what happens. Did it work as intended? If not, iterate – don't be afraid to change course as the facts change.

- Maintain a learning mindset, so that you don't resist or ignore signals to change course.

YOUR TURN

1. Have a look at your agency's press clippings. If you're not already on the circulation list for them, ask your media team if they can sign you up. It's a quick and easy way to keep yourself informed of what the world thinks of your agency.

   If you can't get press clippings, go to the homepage of your local newspaper.

   Peruse the top couple of stories and look for the what's-so statements. These are usually the statements up front. You'll recognise them because they tend to have numbers or descriptors in them.

   For example, "The accused is a 25-year-old white male" or "The Premier made her remarks from Parliament House," or "Temperatures reached a record 46 degrees".

2. Now look for some design statements – those statements of how things should be. Are people disagreeing about how things should be? Disagreement is especially likely when the article involves comments by a government minister, because they will usually also include a comment from the opposition – and they always disagree with each other.

3. Now look for the commentary around delivery. Are the players talking about what they will do or what they have done? Are they talking about successes or failures? Most newspaper articles discuss only three things from governments – conflict, commitments and cock-ups. So unless it's a dry suburban paper (or a paper shilling for the government) you're unlikely to find anything that talks about successful project delivery. But you'll almost certainly find an article that describes project failures!

Conclusion

The journey of a thousand miles begins at your feet.

Chinese proverb

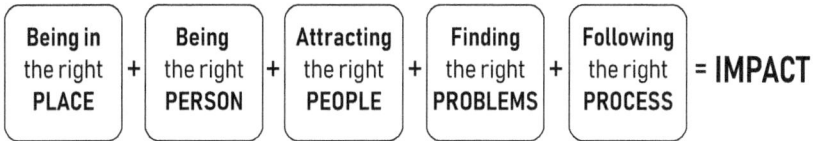

| Being in the right PLACE | + | Being the right PERSON | + | Attracting the right PEOPLE | + | Finding the right PROBLEMS | + | Following the right PROCESS | = IMPACT |

You made it!

That's a big deal. I mean it. Finding time to do anything these days is hard, so for you to have read this entire book is an achievement. You care enough about your job, your world and yourself to have invested the time.

Now it's time to invest a little bit more, by putting everything you've read into practice. I know you've already started, so keep going.

I promised you at the beginning of this book that I'd teach you simple ideas that would change how you approach your job. I want to remind you of them now.

In Part 1 we learned about why the public sector is the *right place*. We explored **needs versus wants, service delivery versus regulation, the seven Public Sector Principles** and the **ESE model**.

Part 2 gave you tools to grow yourself into the *right person*. You drew your **Ikigai**, saw the difference between **success, power** and **impact**, became a **synthesiser** and learned how to avoid becoming **toxic waste**.

Part 3 showed you how to attract the *right people* by exploring your **stakeholders**, using the **HEAT Sheet** and **HEAT Map** to build your **coalitions of support**, and uncovered why **social license** is so important.

In Part 4 we explored how to find the *right problems* by exploring what **disruptions** mean for your work, how to **foresee** them, and then find **solvable problems worth solving**.

And finally, in Part 5 we brought it all together. **The Fairness Delta** lets you bring together everything I've taught you to **discover**, **design** and **deliver** gap-closing projects that the citizens of your jurisdiction will respect.

GOOD ENOUGH

Designing without doing is dreaming. So if the lessons in this book are to improve you, **you must practise them**.

There's actually not that much to learn, you simply have to develop the dexterity to use each tool to its full potential. The only way to do that is to use them, often.

Mozart had access to the same 88 ivory keys as I've got on the piano in my office. But he's a titan of classical music, while I can only butcher "Chopsticks".

"Mozart had a gift!" True. But he also practised a lot more than I do. We can't all be the Mozart of closing gaps. But do we need to be? No, we do not.

When it comes to making change, **being good is truly good enough**.

MY FINAL WORD

You're operating inside a large machine called Government, with many levers of control and persuasion open to you. This book has been written to teach you how to pull the levers at your disposal to achieve real impact in the world.

But a book is only worth so much. As the saying goes, you can lead a horse to water but you can't make it drink.

So, it's up to you now. Drink – or don't.

But know this – no matter who you are, what your background, your rank, role, tenure or team constraints, you CAN have impact on the things that matter to you.

And if you practise on small things now, you WILL grow. You WILL be recognised. You WILL get bigger and bigger challenges. You WILL be uncomfortable, because growing is uncomfortable. But you WILL make the world far better than if you'd done nothing.

I want you to feel zero pressure to fix everything, but all the pressure to try fixing *something*. When it comes to building a wonderful world, as UK grocer Tesco says, **every little helps**.

And in a few years when you feel you've mastered all the tools in this book, come see me again. I've got a cabinet full of power tools I haven't shown you yet. They're how you'll go from fixing the scale of problems you're facing today, to the bigger, hairier ones of tomorrow.

I'd like my very last words to you to be these. I am so proud of you. I am so grateful to you for dedicating your energy to making our shared world better. Thank you. **You are the future, and the future is bright.**

I'd love to hear how you go, so jump onto www.upsides.com.au or connect with me on LinkedIn and keep me posted.

You've got this,

Georgie

Glossary

User note: any bold definitions have been taken from Miriam Webster Dictionary online. Any non-bold definitions are the author's own.

Term	Definition	1st used (Ch)
Agency	The organisation you work for. May be a department, authority, agency, bureau, office or dozens of other names.	1
Attitude	3rd component of *HEAT*. The measure of the extent to which a stakeholder thinks well or poorly of the problem or the project.	13
Bottom line	The total of all costs paid by and revenue earned by a company in delivering its products or services to the market. Excludes *externalities*.	6
Bureaucracy	**1. A body of non-elected government officials.** 2. Referring to the totality of the laws and rules made by governments. 3. A derogatory word for difficult governmental processes.	1

Term	Definition	1st used (Ch)
Citizen	1. A native or naturalized person who owes allegiance to a government and is entitled to protection from it. 2. Any human or non-human resident of a *jurisdiction*. Depending on the context, this can include inanimate objects such as waterways, as well as ideas such as the economy.	1
Common good	Similar to the *public good*; matters which are to the advantage of the whole of a system, including human and non-human interests.	6
Compile	Step 2 of the *synthesiser* process. Allowing the information gained in the *sample* step to be processed by your subconscious brain.	10
Compliance	1. Conformity in fulfilling official requirements. 2. The extent to which your target stakeholder is doing what you need them to do, e.g. signing up to your newsletter, driving on the right side of the road etc.	2
Deliver	Step 3 of the *Delta change model*; execute your plan to get where you're going.	22
Delta (change model)	The basic three-step architecture of all change – *discover, design, deliver*.	22
Design	Step 2 of the *Delta change model*; decide where you're going and how you're getting there.	22

Term	Definition	1st used (Ch)
Discover	Step 1 of the *Delta change model*; establish where you're at.	22
Disruption	A moment of change, upheaval and moving away from the old way of doing things. Disruptions trigger changes to government processes. Citizens expect governments to foresee and respond favourably to disruptions as they emerge.	Part 4 intro
Duty holder	See *target*.	4
Edit	Step 3 of the *synthesiser* process. The conscious process of analysing the information gathered in the *sample* step, with the benefit of any subconscious insights generated during the *compile* step.	10
Engagement	2nd component of *HEAT*. The measure of the extent to which a stakeholder is paying attention to the problem or project.	13
ESE Model	A model illustrating the relationship between the economy, human society and the environment. The ESE Model reminds us that the economy depends on society depends on the environment. When one sphere's activities push beyond their natural limits, the consequences are felt in the next sphere up.	6
Expedience	The act of making decisions based on what is convenient or easy, or of failing to make difficult decisions and thus letting the status quo dictate outcomes (contrast with *principle*).	5

Term	Definition	1st used (Ch)
Externality	Costs generated by a business but paid for by someone or something else, e.g. pollution, human health impacts.	6
Goals	(as in *success, power, impact*) The measures of *success*.	8
Goods	Opposite of *services*. Tangible. Material items provided to recipients.	1
HEAT	Refers to *heft, engagement, attitude, trigger*.	13
Heft	1st component of *HEAT*. The measure of the extent to which a stakeholder wields influence over the problem or the project.	13
Ikigai	A Japanese concept involving personal reflection on four elements that together produce a state of harmonious alignment of one's efforts with one's work. Ikigai asks individuals to examine their *talent, joy, income* and *service* needs.	7
Impact	(as in *success, power, impact*) Improving what matters, as defined by you or someone else.	8
Income	Element 3 of *Ikigai*. Asks the individual to reflect on the amount of money required to meet one's needs and desired standard of living.	7

Term	Definition	1st used (Ch)
Institutional memory	The totality of what the people within your *agency* know, including law and policies, as well as practices, culture, history and subject knowledge relating to the administration of its remit. Institutional memory is held in the minds of the staff and in enshrined processes, and is susceptible to erosion through staff cuts, under-resourcing or other large disruptions. Institutional memory has positives and negatives. For example, loss of institutional memory – a hiring freeze can lead to reduced performance, whereas too much institutional memory can lead to stagnation and the preservation of "that's the way it's always been done" ism.	5
Joy	Element 2 of *Ikigai*. Asks the individual to reflect on what they gain pleasure from doing.	7
Jurisdiction	**1. The limits or territory within which authority may be exercised.** 2. The reach of your *agency*, meaning both its territory and its *remit*.	Part 1 intro
Level	(as in level of government) Refers to whether an *agency* is at the federal, state or local level.	Part 1 intro
Low-hanging fruit	A colloquial term referring to improvements that have a high value-for-effort ratio. AKA quick wins, no-brainers.	22
Non-excludable	A *good* or *service* available to all *citizens*.	1

Term	Definition	1st used (Ch)
Non-rivalrous	A *good* or *service* that doesn't reduce in supply as it's consumed.	1
Obligatee	See *target*.	12
Playback	Step 4 of the *synthesiser* process. The final step, whereby you first craft then tell the story of the issue you've been synthesising, with a view to gaining support for action.	10
Portfolio	The *agency* or cluster of agencies you work for – I worked for the Environment Protection Authority, which was part of the environment portfolio with two other agencies. Some common portfolios are health, corrective services, emergency services or finance.	Part 1 intro
Power	(as in *success, power, impact*) Defining *success*, for yourself or others.	8
Principle	A defining belief or value that can be used to frame decisions in a way that accords with generally accepted ideas of rightness and/or fairness (contrast with *expedience*). See the public sector principles (Chapter 2).	5
Private good	An individual want that is met by provision of a *good* or *service* provided by private sector entities (companies). Contrast with *public good*.	1
Private sector	**The part of an economy which is not controlled or owned by the government.**	Part 1 intro

Term	Definition	1st used (Ch)
Privatisation	The transfer of public functions from public to private sector delivery, either through sale, tender/contracts or long-term leasing. Example of sale: the privatisation of Telstra happened when the Commonwealth Telecommunication Service (Telecomm, rebranded Telstra) was sold on the public market in tranches in the 1990s. Example of tender: Melbourne's train network infrastructure is still state-owned, however operations of the train service are provided by the private sector and awarded through periodic tender processes. Example of leasing: most mines in Australia are operated by private companies on Crown land. Once the company has the lease it is generally not re-negotiated, unlike a tender/contract.	1
Problem statement	The succinct statement of what your project is designed to solve.	22
Public good	A *good* or *service* that benefits society as a whole, which is made available to all members of a society (sometimes with conditions). Due to their *non-excludable*, *non-rivalrous* nature, access to public goods is typically administered by governments and paid for via taxation.	1
Public sector	A broad term referring to both *public service* agencies, public enterprises (e.g. government-owned corporations), and other government-funded entities such as schools and hospitals.	Intro

Term	Definition	1st used (Ch)
Public service	Used in this book to refer to the *agencies* that deliver most public administrative functions. A subset of the *public sector*.	Part 1 intro
Recipient	A person receiving the service provided by a *public sector agency*.	2
Regenerative capitalism	An economic model that applies laws of nature to socioeconomic systems, with the goal of replacing the dominant economic model with one more compatible with the continuation and extension of human living standards on planet Earth.	19
Regulatee	See *target*.	12
Regulation	The act of delivering services that are needed but not necessarily wanted by the recipient.	2
Regulatory agency	An *agency* tasked with delivering *regulation*.	2
Remit	The scope of your *agency's* work. Your *agency's* "job".	1
S-curve	A mathematical graph that establishes the pattern of cumulative growth over time.	21
Sample	Step 1 of the *synthesiser* process. Gather relevant facts and opinions from stakeholders. This material becomes the "feedstock" for the remainder of the process.	10
Service	Element 4 of *Ikigai*. Asks the individual to reflect on the way in which they wish to be of service to the world. Can be used in conjunction with the *ESE Model*.	7

Term	Definition	1st used (Ch)
Service delivery	The act of delivering *services* that are both needed and wanted (or the *agency* responsible for the delivery).	2
Service delivery agency	An *agency* tasked with *service delivery*.	2
Services	Opposite of *goods*. Intangible amenities, benefits or facilities provided to recipients.	1
Social license	Ongoing acceptance of an entity and its practices by its *stakeholders*.	11
Stakeholder	**One who is involved in or affected by a course of action.**	10
Success	(as in *success, power, impact*) Reaching goals set for you, e.g. Key Performance Indicators.	8
Synthesiser	A 4-step process to *sample, compile, edit* and *playback*. Synthesis is akin to being a "clearing house" for information and ideas. Practitioners collect multiple streams of information, reprocess it to gain insight, then share the results to others with a view to gaining support for action.	10
Talent	Element 1 of *Ikigai*. Asks the individual to reflect on what they're good at doing, based on their knowledge and skills.	7
Target	A person or class of people whose behaviour you're seeking to control or change.	12

Term	Definition	1st used (Ch)
Taxpayer	Someone who pays taxes to a given jurisdiction.	4
Trigger	4th component of *HEAT*. The topic/s that are held dear by the stakeholder; the lever/s that might allow a project manager to improve a stakeholder's engagement or attitude.	13
Triple bottom line	An accounting term referring to three categories of costs or benefits: economic, social and environmental.	1
User	1. The people who receive the benefit of your service, or 2. subject of your controlling legislation (in regulation), or 3. the beneficiaries of your controlling legislation.	12

Endnotes

Part 1: PLACE. The stuff you won't get taught at work (but should)

1. Hopkins, D. R. (2002). *The Greatest Killer: Smallpox in History.* University of Chicago Press.

2. World Health Organization. (1980). *World Health: the magazine of the World Health Organization.* May 1980.

Chapter 1: Why every civilisation creates governments

1. I'll use the term "public good" in this chapter. But in Chapter 6 I'll expand it to "common good", which is even better.

2. And that's why I put a streetlight on the cover of this book.

3. Clean Energy Report Australia 2015, Clean Energy Council.

Chapter 3: You can't do that! Know where your power comes from

1. Sourced from the Federal Register of Legislation at 19 January 2022. For the latest information on Australian Government law please go to https://www.legislation.gov.au.

Chapter 4: There is no customer

1. "Citizen" might be defined narrowly or broadly – somebody who holds a passport of your country versus somebody who lives in your town.

Chapter 6: Triple bottom line versus the real world

1. Asana. (2021). Australia and New Zealand Anatomy of Work Index 2021.

2. Rushkoff, D. (2022). "The super-rich 'preppers' planning to save themselves from the apocalypse". Retrieved from *The Guardian*: https://www.theguardian.com/news/2022/sep/04/super-rich-prepper-bunkers-apocalypse-survival-richest-rushkoff.

Part 2: PERSON. You're the best tool you'll ever have; wield yourself wisely

Chapter 7: Map your motivations with Ikigai

1. A 360 Review is a formal feedback gathering tool that seeks input from people who surround you – peers, supervisors, clients and subordinates (i.e., 360 degrees). The feedback is generally anonymous. You'll get scored on a long list of standardised criteria. Crucially, it asks you to review yourself as well, so you can assess whether your self-perception lines up with others' perception of you. 360s can be scary, but they're also crazy useful, so whenever you get the chance, do it.

2. FI/RE = Financial Independence, Retire Early. It's a thing.

3. There is an industry full of people who will happily give you money advice – especially if you pay them. It's not why I'm writing this book but let me give you one piece of wealth advice while I've got you. Save half of every pay rise. That's it. It's the easiest savings strategy you'll ever find; you won't notice the money's missing because you never had it before. If you can get to financial independence, you can then pursue work for its own

sake, not for money. It's a lot easier to find work that satisfies three spheres instead of four.

Chapter 9: How not to turn into a toxic waste

1. Rohn, J., https://www.jimrohn.com. Accessed July 2022.

2. Free life lesson – this applies in your personal life just as much as at work. Choose your friends carefully, and if you don't like the direction your life is heading, start by finding different friends.

3. https://www.qld.gov.au/jobs/finding/interviews

4. https://www.careerone.com.au/career-advice/career/how-to-prepare-for-a-public-sector-interview-2709

Chapter 10: How to become a synthesiser

1. Walker, M. P. (2009). "The Role of Sleep in Cognition and Emotion". *The Year in Cognitive Neuroscience 2009* (1156), pp168–197.

   Bos, M. W., Dijksterhuis, A., & van Baaren, R. B. (2011). "The benefits of "sleeping on things": Unconscious thought leads to automatic weighting". *Journal of Consumer Psychology*, 21(1), 4-8. doi:https://doi.org/10.1016/j.jcps.2010.09.002

   Cote, K. A., Lustig, K. A., & MacDonald, K. J. (2019). Chapter 33 – The Role of Sleep in Processing Emotional Information. In Elsevier, & H. C. Dringenberg (Ed.), *Handbook of Behavioral Neuroscience* (pp. 505-518). doi:https://doi.org/10.1016/B978-0-12-813743-7.00033-5

   Jones, S., Castelnovo, A., Riedner, B., Flaherty, B., Prehn-Kristensen, A., Benca, R., Tononi, G., Herringa, R. (2021). "Sleep and emotion processing in paediatric posttraumatic stress disorder: A pilot investigation". *Journal of Sleep Research*. doi:https://doi.org/10.1111/jsr.13261

2. "Baseline" is one of those terms that you've either heard a thousand times, or never at all. Baseline refers to the starting point of a situation; how things are before you take any action to change matters. Baselining is important because without a baseline, you'll never know what kind of impact you've had.

    Some things are easy to baseline – how many days does the average patient remain on your ward, or how many tram services are delayed on the #57 route each weekday. Other things are harder to baseline – how easy is it for people to find the fire exits in an emergency, or what feelings do women have when they first learn they're pregnant.

Part 3: PEOPLE. Because even Superman has the Justice League

Chapter 11: Why social license matters

1. In apartheid South Africa, purple became the colour of revolution, whereas Ukraine's 2004 revolution was bathed in orange. In Los Angeles, wearing blue (Crip) or red (Blood) can get you arrested or shot.

2. Skinner, G. (2019). "It's a fact! Scientists are the most trusted people in world". Retrieved from Ipsos MORI: https://www.ipsos.com/ipsos-mori/en-uk/its-fact-scientists-are-most-trusted-people-world

    McCarthy, N. (2019). "America's Most & Least Trusted Professions". Retrieved from Forbes: https://www.forbes.com/

sites/niallmccarthy/2019/01/11/americas-most-least-trusted-professions-infographic/?sh=5a003fe57e94

Australian Council of Professions. (2019). "The Most and Least Trusted Professions in Australia 2019". Retrieved from Professions: https://www.professions.org.au/the-most-and-least-trusted-professions-australia-2019/

3. The Ethics Centre. (2018). "Ethics Explainer: Social license to operate". Retrieved from The Ethics Centre: https://ethics.org.au/ethics-explainer-social-license-to-operate/

4. Public Service Board. (1973). "Hi! Come and join us in Canberra". Canberra, ACT, Australia: Public Service Board.

Chapter 12: These are the people in your neighbourhood

1. Some countries think even longer term. Japan has a 100-year plan to win the Football World Cup. China has a 100-year plan to become a superpower.

2. Think Medicare, same sex marriage or the repeal of the White Australia Policy.

Chapter 16: How to attract the right people to your side

1. Bose, N., & Sgroi, D. (2022). *Small Talk and Theory of Mind in Strategic Decision-Making*. University of Warwick.

Part 4: PROBLEMS. Learn how to spot 'em, scope 'em and box 'em in (so they don't squash you)

1. Arbib, J. & Seba, T. (2020). *Rethinking Humanity*. RethinkX, p42.

Chapter 17: People expect governments to manage disruptions

1. Uber isn't alone – there's Lyft, Ola, Curb, Gett, DiDi… We're focusing on Uber because it was the first.

Chapter 18: The mega-trends driving disruption

1. If reading a report doesn't appeal, check out the 32-minute *Rethinking Humanity* video available on YouTube. Arbib, J. & Seba, T. (2020). *Rethinking Humanity*, RethinkX.

2. Conspiracy of Love. (2022). The Future of Good Report.

Chapter 19: A whistle-stop tour of the most relevant global disruptions

1. Naughtin, C., Hajkowicz, S., Schleiger, E., Bratanova, A., Cameron, A., Zamin, T., & Dutta, A. (2022). "Our Future World: Global megatrends impacting the way we live". Brisbane: CSIRO.

2. Carolo, L. (2020). "3D Printed Shoes in 2020: Big Brands Are on Board". Retrieved from All3DP.com: https://all3dp. com/2/3d-printed-shoes/

3. Carpenter, S. (2021). "The Race To Develop Plastic-Eating Bacteria". Retrieved from Forbes.com: https://www.forbes .com/sites/scottcarpenter/2021/03/10/the-race-to-develop-plastic-eating-bacteria/?sh=23326e447406

4. Tubb, C. & Seba, T. (2019). "Rethinking Food and Agriculture 2020-2030". RethinkX. Retrieved from https://www.rethinkx. com/food-and-agriculture#food-and-agriculture-download

5. Naughtin, C., Hajkowicz, S., Schleiger, E., Bratanova, A., Cameron, A., Zamin, T., & Dutta, A. (2022). "Our Future World: Global megatrends impacting the way we live". Brisbane: CSIRO.

6. Idzelis, C. (2020). "AI-Powered Hedge Funds Vastly Outperformed, Research Shows". Retrieved from Institutional Investor: https://www.institutionalinvestor.com/article/b1mssrswn1mpr0/AIPowered-Hedge-Funds-Vastly-Outperformed-Research-Shows

7. Arbib, J. & Seba, T. (2020). *Rethinking Humanity*, RethinkX.

8. Throughout the Western world, the loss of manufacturing jobs is contributing to reduced rates of marriage, fertility and children born in wedlock. This sets up intergenerational disadvantage and has led to the rise of such phenomena as the Men's Rights movement and populist leaders such as Donald Trump. The right government interventions can arrest this trend.

    Autor, D., Dorn, D., & Hanson, G. (2017). "When Work Disappears: Manufacturing Decline and the Falling Marriage-Market Value of Young Men". Cambridge, Massachusetts: National Bureau of Economic Research.

9. Wunderman Thompson Intelligence. (2020). The Future 100.

10. Dozens of jurisdictions around the world have pothole reporting apps, including the ability to upload photos and add GPS coordinates.

11. A personal favourite and one close to my heart – EPA Victoria has an award-winning app that lets citizens dob on drivers who flick cigarette butts out the car window (a major cause of

bushfires in hot Aussie summers). I've used this app dozens of times to trigger hefty fines to litterbugs.

12. Apps such as Citizen seek to make crime reporting data visible in real time to users. Concerns abound, from vigilantism to racial profiling. But usage is steadily increasing.

13. The Commonwealth of Australia. (2021). The intergenerational Report. Canberra.

14. Edelman. (2020). 20th Annual Edelman Trust Barometer.

15. In fact, expand. Roughly 10 per cent of the global population still live in extreme poverty. There's a moral argument that we in the West have a responsibility to help them climb out of poverty cleanly. After all, they're not the ones who used up all of our planetary headroom.

16. https://www.wa.gov.au/organisation/department-of-the-premier-and-cabinet/collie-just-transition

Chapter 20: Global disruptions affect local lives

1. From Wikipedia: Six Degrees of Kevin Bacon is a game where players challenge each other to arbitrarily choose an actor and then connect them to another actor via a film that both actors have appeared in together, repeating this process to try to find the shortest path that leads to prolific American actor Kevin Bacon.

Chapter 21: How to see disruptions coming

1. 33,554,432 to be precise. Don't believe me? Prove it to yourself – open a spreadsheet and type "1" in cell A1. Then enter this formula into cell A2 "=A1*2". Then copy that same

formula into the next 24 rows and you'll get 33,554,432. I'm as shocked as you.

Chapter 22: How to turn disruptions into problems (you can solve)

1. IMO the best explainer on the whole Cynefin Framework is in a Harvard Business Review article written in 2007 by the Framework's authors, David J. Snowden and Mary E. Boone. Find it here: https://hbr.org/2007/11/a-leaders-framework-for-decision-making. I suggest this article, rather than www.cynefin.io, because the Cynefin website makes little sense if you haven't done the training.

2. This is a misquote – the grenade bit is mine. Given the rampant misquoting in the world, I don't feel too bad about it. But I still feel compelled to point it out to you and beg forgiveness.

Additional references

Australian Industry Group (AiGroup). (2020). Labour Turnover in 2020.

Australian Industry Group (AiGroup). (2021). Labour Turnover in 2021.

Australian Institute of Health and Welfare. (2021). Autism in Australia. Retrieved from Australian Institute of Health and Welfare: https://www.aihw.gov.au/reports/disability/autism-in-australia/contents/autism

Black, J. (2014). *Learning from Regulatory Disasters*. London: London School of Economics and Political Science.

Braithwaite, J. (2011). "The Essence of Responsive Regulation". *UBC Law Review*, 44(3), 475-520.

Brunetto, Y., Shacklock, K., Teo, S., & Farr-Wharton, R. (n.d.). "The impact of management on the engagement and well-being of high emotional labour employees". *The International Journal of Human Resource Management*, 25(17), 2345-2363.

Chughtai, A., Byrne, M., & Flood, B. (2015). "Linking Ethical Leadership to Employee Well-Being: The Role of Trust in Supervisor". *Journal of Business Ethics*, 128, 653–663.

Coglianese, C. (2015). "Listening, Learning, Leading: A Framework for Regulatory Excellence". Philadelphia: University of Pennsylvania Law School.

Gilbreath, B., & Benson, P. (2004). "The contribution of supervisor behaviour to employee psychological well-being". *Work & Stress*, 18(3), 255-266.

Goh, Z., Ilies, R., & Schwind Wilson, K. (2015). "Supportive supervisors improve employees' daily lives: The role supervisors play in the impact of daily workload on life satisfaction via work–family conflict". *Journal of Vocational Behavior*, 89, 65-73.

Government of Victoria. (2014). Victorian Guide to Regulation Toolkit 1: purposes and types of regulation. Melbourne: Department of Treasury and Finance.

McKinsey Centre for Government. (2013). Revolutionary Regulators. McKinsey & Co.

Ochmann, S., & Roser, M. (n.d.). Smallpox. (University of Oxford) Retrieved from Our World In Data: https://ourworldindata.org/smallpox#costs-of-smallpox-and-its-eradication

OECD. (2014). Regulatory Enforcement and Inspections. In OECD, OECD Best Practice Principles for Regulatory Policy. OECD Publishing.

OECD. (2014). The Governance of Regulators. In OECD, Best Practice Principles for Regulatory Policy. OECD Publishing.

OECD Council on Regulatory Policy and Governance. (2012). Recommendation of the Council on Regulatory Policy and Governance. OECD Publishing.

Reb, J., Narayanan, J., & Chaturvedi, S. (2014). "Leading Mindfully: Two Studies on the Influence of Supervisor Trait Mindfulness on Employee Well-Being and Performance". *Mindfulness*, 5, 36–45.

Sparrow, M. K. (2000). *The Regulatory Craft*. Washington DC: The Brookings Institution.

Wingard, J. (2019). "The Patagonia Model: CEOs Redefine Shareholder Value". Retrieved from Forbes.com: https://www.forbes.com/sites/jasonwingard/2019/08/23/the-patagonia-model-ceos-redefine-shareholder-value/?sh=4121278d16e3